Out of EGYPT
The Lord Called

by Greg Taylor

A Study of Leviticus

OUT OF EGYPT: THE LORD CALLED

A Study of Leviticus

Cover design by Nyasha Peters and Greg Taylor
Interior text design by Sandy Armstrong, Strong Design

*"When Israel was a child, I loved him,
and out of Egypt I called my son."*

Hosea 11:1 NIV

Dedication

For Shepherds of The Journey

Table of Contents

CHAPTER 1

The Lord Calls Us Back in Time

Going Back in Time

MY WIFE AND I ONCE TOOK OUR THREE CHILDREN TO Williamsburg, Virginia to see the old town. As we crossed a bridge from the visitor's center to Williamsburg, we passed signs telling us we were going back in time. It was the closest thing I've ever experienced to a time machine.

The sign read something like this: It is now 1940, and you have no computer or cell phone. We passed another sign. 1900: women cannot vote. You've never seen an automobile. Finally, before entering the old town was a sign reading, 1779: You are entering Williamsburg.

When we arrived, we talked with blacksmiths, cobblers, book binders, bakers, brick makers, and silversmiths who all stayed in character throughout our visit.

In order to reach the world of Leviticus, we would continue on an imaginary path further back in time. 1350: Europe is crushed by the black death. 300: Rome collapses. 30: Jesus walks the earth.

Now the steps take you into time before Jesus Christ. 500 BC: rebuilding the Jewish Temple. 1000 BC: Saul anointed Israel's first king. 1400 BC: God frees Israel from slavery and calls them into the wilderness, the setting of Leviticus.

One of the problems with understanding ancient Bible texts is that we are so far removed from them. So we have stepped back in time in order to put ourselves more into the story.

We've walked back in time to the approximate date of the establishment of Israel and the events described in Leviticus. You no longer know what a cell phone is. Your computer is your brain and digits are on your hands. Animals are your property and valuable to you, as is salt, oil, and grains from the fields. Your people have left Egypt and are on a journey to the Promised Land.

We're so happy to be free, but we wonder what's next? Moses is hearing the word of the Lord and repeating those words to us. The book of Leviticus tells the story about what God has to say to His people about what's next after they come Out of Egypt.

What language does God speak?

When I was nineteen, I studied and traveled internationally. My fellow students and I were based outside of Florence, Italy, in a villa in Tuscany. Italians taught us to say what Tuscany and its people were: "Bella." *Beautiful.* Two sweet Italians named Miranda and Renata fed us tortellini and lasagna.

They cooked lunch and dinner, but breakfast was on our own. I was paid work study to be "breakfast boy" of our college group and faculty. We ate hard bread, jam, and drank lattes. Each morning, I made a big pot of cafe latte for a crowd, and this was in the 1980s, before lattes were cool.

As we traveled, our faculty taught us much about what we were seeing. We visited ancient Roman ruins, the Eiffel Tower, paintings in museums and cathedrals. Knowing what we knew, we still often shrugged and walked on. One of our fellow students named Wayne said he had a photographic memory, so he carried no camera, just drank it all in. Indeed, he may have remembered more by viewing the world not through a camera lens but through the naked eye.

We traveled to Paris, Munich, Strasburg, Amsterdam, Rome, but mostly what we did was eat. Italian gelato— Stracciatella and Fragola to be exact. Did our faculty sponsors want to shoot us in the neck with tranquilizer darts and replace us with students who cared more about art and less about gelato? Likely.

In the midst of this toggling between "learning" and gelato, I truly learned something very important that changed my life. I won't forget the smallish old domed church house where this became clear. Our student group attended a worship service in Italian. No translation. If we wanted to "get something out of it," we were going to have to strain to hear the bits of Italian we had been learning.

That was the day and the place I realized this: **God doesn't speak English**. Well, I have no doubt He can speak English, but I never imagined that God spoke anything *but* English. Worse further, till then I imagined God needed to be spoken to in King James English. "Thou" and "Thy" were considered the only proper and holy ways to refer to God. But these, I learned in Italy, were only old English ways of referring to God. God had spoken and was spoken to in many languages for many centuries, and English was a relatively new language for communicating with God!

What is Leviticus Anyway?

So, what language did God speak in the world of Leviticus? Hebrew.

Hebrew is read from right to left. Even the titles in the Hebrew Bible are different from our English translations. Leviticus is not titled Leviticus or even a Hebrew equivalent. Hebrew titles are typically the same as the first word of text. In this case the first line of text in Leviticus is **wayyiqrā'**, which means "He [the Lord] called."

Over the centuries of translations, eventually the title changed. English followed the lead of Latin and Greek translations that attempted to give titles that described the contents. Therefore, the English title Leviticus is a transliteration of Latin and Greek titles, and it means, "Instructions to the Levites."

Do not, however, let the name Leviticus mislead you, because the original title in Hebrew is the beginning of the first line of text that goes on to say that "the Lord called Moses." That is why this book is titled, "Out of Egypt: The Lord Called."

Leviticus is the story about how Moses was called by God, and then Moses was told to call Israel to worship and serve the One Holy God who led them out of Egypt and into a life of freedom and holiness.

Is Leviticus Only for Jews and Levites?

Is this book only for Israel? Even more narrowly, is Leviticus written for people like Aaron, Moses' brother who was the first priest? Wasn't it just laws about how to worship God that are now done away with after Jesus died on the cross?

Does Leviticus and the words God spoke through Moses to Aaron, the Levites, and Israel still matter today?

First, not all Levites were priests. They were all from the Levite tribe but not all in the tribe were priests. Second, while Leviticus 1-16 is addressed to the Levite priests and their ritual practices in the tabernacle, the second half is addressed to all of Israel. Furthermore, I believe Leviticus is not just a call for the Levites and Israel: God is calling us to be holy today. By walking in the shoes of the first people God called, we get a clearer picture of what has been important to God since ancient times.

So, be transported not only in time and in this study but in your heart and imagination as you contemplate these ancient passages, see them through the lenses of the original recipients, and decide for yourself how relevant they are for our lives today.

The Lord is calling. He is calling us to understand what it has meant for more than three millennia to be the holy people of God. God is not calling only ancients but he is also calling us today. Will we listen?

Why does Leviticus Still Matter?

One of my favorite books is by Eric Schlosser, *Fast Food Nation*. The book remains one of the twentieth century's most influential books about the underbelly of American consumerism.

In one of the most vivid chapters, Schlosser describes going to a slaughterhouse in Iowa and seeing factory butchers knee deep in blood of cows and pigs.

Americans get our meat in clean packages that look nothing like an animal. We have removed ourselves from the stench of blood and guts. Ranchers and meat packers mass produce meat as if it was a factory product. Millions of animals are unceremoniously slaughtered every year in America so many of us who rarely see a cow or chicken can have daily nuggets and burgers.

What does this have to do with Leviticus? To prepare you for reading Leviticus, you ought to know that animal slaughter is discussed, and we will get into that later. But for now, suffice it to say that Schlosser's book has to do with Leviticus because one of the objections of reading Leviticus is that it's gross. I've even heard people say how grateful they are that we don't live in the world of Leviticus, slaughtering all those animals.

Excuse me but, "we" do slaughter animals today. Our society slaughters many more animals today than ancient Israel did. If you read *Fast Food Nation* side by side with Leviticus, you would likely choose Leviticus as the cleaner book to read, the book that would let you sleep more soundly, and *Fast Food Nation* would be the book more likely to convert you to a vegan.

So then, what if processing meat today is less humane and civil than the Israelite method described in Leviticus?

Human life, animal life and blood are all very important to God. Leviticus describes the process of bringing life into God's presence and keeping sacred everything related to killing, eating, property, worship, sexual life. Meanwhile, today we have secularized and commercialized slaughter of animals, dehumanized nameless bodies in a sea of pornography, and become desperately distant from one another rather than living in communities like Israel did.

I'm not suggesting that we practice Israelite customs, but we certainly have much to learn about God and sacred living from a study of Leviticus. This is one of the reasons Leviticus still matters today.

No More Avoiding Leviticus!

Gross description of animal slaughter is *the* reason middle school age boys might read Leviticus, but it remains one of the reasons people avoid reading the book. Not only that but many people avoid reading Leviticus because it is repetitive and contains some strange ideas. Whether you've tried to read Leviticus zero times, once, or ten times, you probably hit a brick wall at this third book of the Old Testament.

I call it the "Wall of Leviticus." You can't get around it, can't go under it, can't scale it. You have to break through it. This study is for those who have never broken through Leviticus. It's also for those who want to help others in their small group or church to break through to its importance.

What you are holding in your hands is not a detailed commentary of every line in Leviticus. The text of Leviticus alone is nearly as long as this entire book. Rather than verse by verse commentary, this book provides a teacher's or participant's guide to reading the text. Since we've missed or skipped Leviticus so many years, we have a lot of catching up to do.

If you've avoided reading Leviticus because of the cultural distance of three thousand years, it's gross, repetitive, and contains strange ideas, you will find in this book a whole new way to think about Leviticus.

Some of the most potent principles of the Israelite faith originate in Leviticus. The recurring theme of being holy because God is holy is connected in Leviticus with worship and living of Israel. Leviticus provides us with deep insight into the earliest requirements of God for Israel to become a holy people, about what it means to live in the presence of a holy God and be his chosen nation. The Year of Jubilee, atonement, and scapegoat are all first fully described in Leviticus (16:1f; 25:1f).

Leviticus Points to Jesus!

The major difference between our life and Israel's is the work of God in Christ, such as the atonement done through him: Christ's blood has atoned for our sins once and for all (Hebrews 9:28). So we do not, again and again, return to the Tabernacle or Temple to sacrifice. Yet the nature of community, the moral laws of God, the reflection of the image of God in his holiness as his people, all these principles still apply to us as Christians.

Is the Old Testament, Leviticus in particular, authoritative for us? The following from the *New Bible Commentary* helps answer this question.

Jacob Milgram says, "For the Christian, the grace which Leviticus offered through the sacrificial system is now found wholly in Jesus Christ, and the sacrifices provided the New Testament authors with a rich imagery for interpreting the significance of the cross. Likewise, the demand for holiness, in Leviticus a badge of Israel's separation from the nations, is transformed in the New Testament into the call to Christian distinctiveness from the world. But the moral challenge of Leviticus, as of the whole law, cannot be confined to the church. God created Israel to be a light to the nations. Their distinctiveness was to enable them to model the ethical standards and direction of life that God ultimately wants for all. The book thus has important lessons for the understanding of our salvation, our personal sanctification and our social ethics. Leviticus is a part of those Scriptures which, according to Paul, are able to make us wise for salvation and are profitable for teaching us how to live (2 Tim. 3:15–17)."

Should we still practice certain principles or commands of the Old Testament such as commands in Leviticus? Most of us are not very consistent with this: we keep the Ten Commandments, but few Christians feel the need to keep the Sabbath. Some Christians even symbolically celebrate Jewish feasts such as Passover or commemorate Rosh Hashanah or Yom Kippur, but few Christians—or even modern Jews for that matter—would ever sacrifice an animal as a means of cleansing for sin.

The fact is that we all pick and choose those parts of the Bible that are normative for us, but the guiding principle should be the very nature of God—what does our holy God want from us now? Also guiding us is the teaching of Jesus Christ, the Apostles, and the writings of the New Testament. Jesus, Paul, Peter, John—no one called for the repudiation of all forms of Judaism. In fact, Christians were grafted into the Jewish tree, not the reverse (Romans 9).

What we will see in this study over and over is that the most important thing all these words of the Lord point to, in form of festivals, commands, laws governing neighborly relationships is ultimately to have a good relationship between Holy God and Israel.

Reflecting

Read Leviticus 1 and any introductory notes your Bible contains, then reflect with others on the following:

1. What do you *like* about the story?
2. What do you *not like* about story?
3. What do you think the story is saying to the *original audience*?
4. What is the story saying to us *today*?
5. What is the story calling us to *believe*?
6. What is the story calling us to *do*?
7. With whom can you *share* this story this week?

Prayer

God our Father, the blood of bulls and goats—as the Hebrew writer says, can never take away sin, but we have access to the atoning sacrifice of your son, Jesus Christ. He shed blood for us once for all. Transport us into the Israelite world so we can know the desperation of being without Jesus but the peace (Shalom) of knowing you are pursuing us and are present with us.

CHAPTER 2

How Do We Live
With Holy God?

Boundaries for a Holy People

WHEN I WAS A THIRTEEN YEARS OLD GROWING UP IN Oklahoma, I was cutting grass on a neighbor's land. I had been volun-told to mow for these elderly neighbors. As I mowed, I noticed the fencing was not barbed wire but only narrow gauge wire strung from pole to pole with small white metallic connectors. How could that fence hold in a cow?

I cut the mower off and walked over to the fence. I didn't *decide* to touch it but impulsively touched it. That was the moment I learned how this fence could keep cows

19

contained. Volts! The fence was electric. That was my brief education in electric fences. I needed no other course of instruction. Now I knew what it was, that touching it was painful, that I should not repeat this educational experience for a long time.

Leviticus is Israel's education about how to live with the One Holy God of the Universe.

Leviticus tells the fantastic story of Israel's education about how to live in the presence of a holy God. This was no ordinary journey, for in these years the God of the universe made his presence known to Israel in the most striking and shocking ways known to mankind.

Leviticus is also full of voltage for people straying out of the boundaries of God's desires. There are boundaries for the people to stay in the community and honor God, and not return to slavery and idolatry.

How Then Are We to Live?

Leviticus opens with God speaking, instructing his people how to honor him, how to be holy like Himself, how to remain in his presence and reflect his image. Again, the overriding question of Leviticus is this: "In light of God's holy presence, how then are we to live?"

Nearly every section of Leviticus begins with the nameless one—who they called Yahweh—speaking directly to Moses, Israel's leader. Sixteen of the book's twenty-seven chapters begin with the Lord speaking to Moses. Moses in turn communicates these words to Aaron, who had been appointed chief priest over the Levites. The Levities perform the rituals of the new place of God's presence, the Tabernacle. God speaks in the form of a Divine word to a messenger, Moses, who is commissioned to disseminate the oracle to Aaron, the Levite priests, and to all of Israel.

The book before Leviticus in the Pentateuch (Five Books of Law), Exodus, chronicles God's deliverance of Israel out of Egyptian slavery. Where the story of the Exodus ends, the story world of Leviticus begins. In the latter half of Exodus, God is shown dictating the details of the tabernacle tent, enclosure, and furnishings.

Bezalel and Oholiab were to oversee the construction of the Tabernacle. It is likely that other members of the tribe of Dan joined Oholiab, who helped the Spirit-filled Bezalel to craft designs in gold, silver, and bronze, cut and set stone, and to build everything the Lord commanded.

The Lord commanded Bezalel and Oholiab to construct a Tent of Meeting, the ark of the Testimony with the atonement cover on it, and all the other furnishings of the tent, the table and articles, the pure gold lamp stand and accessories, the altar of incense, the altar of burnt offerings and utensils, the basin and stand, the woven garments, both the sacred garments for Aaron the priest and the garments for his sons when they serve as priests, and the anointing oil and fragrant incense for the Holy Place. They are to make them "just as I commanded you" (Ex. 31:7-11).

When He Talks, People Listen

A commercial from the 1980s for E.F. Hutton financial services features a classroom of students who stop what they were doing and lean in, hand cupping their ear toward a person in the class who's telling a friend, "My broker is E.F.Hutton, and he says . . ." The tag line was, "When E.F. Hutton speaks, people listen."

Those who listened to this financial advise could not have been so blessed as those who have listened to God through the ages, for the voice of God has been vital to the identity of our forebears, Israel, and the Christian faith.

The first and most prominent example of God speaking and "others" listening is the stars that were flung into this unfathomable universe by words of the Creator.

All creation listened and obeyed. But after a time, humans sinned and descended into rebellion, the opposite of listening. They were lost and wandering apart from God. What did God do in order for people to again enjoy his presence? The message of Leviticus is an early action that answers this question.

God speaks and people listen.

Such is the speaking and obeying pattern of Leviticus: God speaks and expects his people to listen and obey, even more intently than they listen to financial advice. The first section of text in Leviticus is book-ended with God speaking (1:1) and the Israelites obeying (8:4, 9, 13, 17, 21, 29, 36).

This form is repeated more than two dozen times: "The Lord said to Moses, say to the Israelites (or Aaron) . . ."

The creation of Israel had come, like creation, from the words that proceeded from the mouth of God. Now it was Israel's turn, like creation—the stars—to obey.

God's First Words in Leviticus

God's first words to Moses in Leviticus set the stage for an entire system of sacrificial offerings of the Israelites. Sacrifices, however, were neither new to Israel nor the larger culture. But because of the distance of time and space—remember the journey back in time—we need more explanation of the purpose of sacrifices.

Why sacrifices? Sacrifices represented a vital understanding of atonement: forgiveness comes at the cost of life, the shedding of blood. The sacrifices were a means through which God forgives his people for sins, both intentional and non-intentional, a means of restoring fellowship. Unlike the cultic gods of the contemporary culture to Israel, sacrifices did not equate with "feeding" the God of Israel.

In contrast, these sacrifices were God-commanded not for appeasement but for laying the pathway for his divine presence with them. Sin, we have found in our humanity, is one thing we cannot control or self-forgive. It must be divinely forgiven.

So God's first call to Moses in Leviticus 1 begins what to us may seem like a complicated system of sacrifices and offerings, but these were understood in their world as the means of restoration of relationship: "Speak to the Israelites and say to them: 'When any of you brings an offering to the Lord, bring as your offering an animal from either the herd or flock . . .'" (1:2).

God demands the best of the herd, a male animal without defect for what is called "burnt offerings," which were the most common kind of sacrifice and the first type recorded in Leviticus. The word holocaust is associated with the genocide of Jews in Nazi Germany in the 1930s and 40s. The word, however, also means a sacrifice that is completely burned up. Some Bible translations translate references to burnt offering as the "holocaust offering."

The purpose of the burnt offering was to please God, plain and simple, to be to him "a burnt offering, an offering made by fire, and aroma pleasing to the Lord" (1:9, 13, 17; 2:2, 9, 16; 3:5, 11, 16). Used for either atonement of sins or for thanksgiving worship to God, the most common burnt offerings were animals slaughtered, cut into pieces, and burned completely, except for the hides that belonged to the priests. Animals included cattle, sheep, goats, doves, and pigeons and grain offerings consisted of grains, oil, wine, and frankincense.

Frankincense, one of the spices given to Christ as a gift from the Magi, was strong incense and part of this pleasing aroma to the Lord.

All of the Animal

The most important distinction between mere slaughter of an animal and those given as sacrifice was the sprinkling of the blood on the sides of the altar by the priests, and the portioning of the best parts for the Lord and the priests.

This blood validated the sacrifice, cleansed sins of the person (and household) of the one offering the animal or bird. Provision of sacrifice of birds is made for the poor and the shedding of blood is suspended for the very poor who could only bring a few handfuls of grain for an offering.

Many societies today, and certainly in ancient times, used the entire animal, head to foot: entrails, heart, kidneys, and liver. As they would say in the dust bowl days in Oklahoma, "When slaughtering a pig, use everything but the squeal." It was all good and in some cultures, such as the Basoga in Uganda, the chicken gizzard is considered the choice piece and often offered to guests.

The entrails, kidneys, fat of an animal, therefore, had great value, yet Israel was called to sacrifice this best portion to the Lord. So they offered not only the best from herd, flock, and field, but they were also called upon to offer up to God the very best portions of these by fire, a sweet aroma rising up to the Lord.

We should take note of the fact that the food offered for God is also the food allowed for the human table. What does this say to us? For one thing, it says we are intended to enjoy food together. It says that we reflect God's image.

It says that animals fit for God's table are also fit for Israel's table.

Don't Leave Out the Salt!

I fell in love with salt as a young boy. I remember feeding the cows and watching them slather their thick slimy tongues across the "salt lick," a big block of solid sodium nitrate.

I wanted to try that salt lick. I did not, but I've always enjoyed salt as much as a cow licking that block.

Every family ought to have popcorn, and I happen to be the Taylor family popcorn chef. If there's no proper salt (a lighter, more powdery salt that doesn't bounce off the kernels), then I don't make popcorn. Why dribble huge salt grains off of kernels and watch helplessly as it all falls to the bottom of the pan?

Speaking of the bottom of the pan, I've been known to run my finger across that oil and salt, like a salt lick.

Chapter 2 is about grain offerings. Israel was warned not to leave the salt out of their grain offerings. Salt was a valuable commodity, used in many ancient cultures to barter, considered as valuable as we value money (2:13). Salt also reminded Israel of the covenant between God and his people.

Grain offerings were meant to include the poor or those without herds or flocks (5:7, 11). These were often cakes or breads made with flour, salt, and oil and most often without yeast (2:2-5), but yeast and honey were allowed in the thanksgiving offerings at harvest time (2:11-12).

Part of the offering was considered a memorial portion for the Lord and another portion was given to Aaron and his sons for their food (2:3), presumably as a way to support the ministers of the worship in Israel.

Are You Well?

Thanksgiving is my favorite holiday. The reason is pretty simple. Food. Turkey and dressing (stuffing), and the dressing has cornbread as well as yeast bread. Homemade rolls and pies. Sweet potatoes. Each year we look forward to this holiday to give thanks for all God has done for us.

Another reason I like Thanksgiving best of all is because there is not all the hubbub of Christmas gift exchanges. I don't want to be a Scrooge for the younger generation, but many of us older folks have received enough gifts in our lives, most likely, that we could probably all afford to give ourselves fewer gifts, and needy children more gifts.

If there was a close equivalent to the "Well Being Offering" described in Leviticus 3, at least one the average American can understand, it's the celebration of Thanksgiving. For Israel, thanksgiving for what God has done is one of their first moves in worship.

The Well Being Offering, also called in some translations, "Fellowship Offering," is for the purpose of thanking God for wealth and prosperity, and with that comes the desire to share food with family and friends. So when an Israelite wanted to slaughter an animal, he dedicated it to the Lord in a well-being offering and gave to the Lord a memorial portion.

The Lord speaks of three examples of this well-being offering: cattle, sheep, and goats. The process is the same with each but the ritual is powerful. As with the burnt offering, they are to bring animals without blemish or defect, a reflection on God's image of perfection and his creation and his desire for his people to offer up their very best to him.

Israelites are instructed to offer their best animal, lay their hands on its head, the priests will slaughter it at the entrance of the Tent of Meeting, dash blood on the sides of the altar, remove the entrails, kidneys, and fat portions around the loins and liver, add wood to the altar, and burn the fat portions on the altar to the Lord—they "turned them into smoke."

Fat and blood are not to be eaten, and this is made explicit as a long-term ordinance "throughout your generations, in all your settlements"—a common refrain—"all the fat is the Lord's" and do not eat blood: "This is a lasting ordinance for the generations to come, wherever you live: you must not eat any fat or any blood" (3:17). This, perhaps, is why so few cultures in the world today eat blood. It has become repulsive to us because it was set apart by God as something we were not to consume, because it separates life and death.

The most important point of this chapter is that God established the sacrificial system to purge and cleanse sin and then enacted the festal occasions as extensions of these sacrificial times in order for the community to enjoy the presence of the Lord in feasting and community fellowship.

Reflecting

Read Leviticus 2-3 then reflect with others on the following:

1. What do you *like* about the story?
2. What do you *not like* about story?
3. What do you think the story is saying to the *original audience*?
4. What is the story saying to us *today*?
5. What is the story calling us to *believe*?
6. What is the story calling us to *do*?
7. With whom can you *share* this story this week?

Prayer

Oh Lord, may we come to understand this portion of your story not as mere theatre of the grotesque and ancient. Leviticus is a book we have stumbled over in the past, and we ask you to now make it our own, a book that retains mystery because we do not understand all things, but one that we can now fathom was a part of your divine plan for redeeming your people and setting them apart to be your holy people.

CHAPTER 3

What Do We Do About Sin?

Restorative Justice

MY DAD HAS A GREAT SAYING THAT I OFTEN REPEAT TO our church ministry staff, family members, and to myself. When folks make excuses for not getting a job done, making a mistake, miscommunication, my dad often says, "One excuse is as good as another."

I was reminded of my dad's saying recently when I saw a billboard with a photo of John Wayne's ubiquitous character, still etched in our minds long after his death, with a quote that said, "Don't much like quitters, son."

My dad and John Wayne aren't much for quitters and excuse makers, and neither am I. In fact, that's how humans seemed to be wired. We may make excuses for ourselves, but we're not much on hearing other people's excuses.

When our three children were young and on occasion physically or emotionally busting on each other, we outlawed the use of the phrase, "I didn't mean to." It is simply too easily abused and overused. If you harm someone, does it matter whether or not you meant to? One excuse is as good as another, right? God knows our hearts but humans know actions. Something may need to be done to reconcile the hurt by one, both, or all people involved.

I heard about a school that decided rather than expelling students, they would seek restorative justice. Expelling a student does what locking up a violent criminal does: it gets them "off the streets" or in the case of school, "out of the halls." Sometimes this is appropriate and necessary, but much of the time young people and adults alike need to face one another and learn to say, "I'm sorry" and make amends. Those are elements of restorative justice.

In restorative justice, the focus is on outcomes between the two or more parties involved. Rather than simply sending people away, people are brought together to discuss the situation with the help of reconcilers, restoring relationship through confession, forgiveness, and a strategy for moving forward in love and fairness.

In ancient Israel, God also provided a way for the people to restore relationship, and Leviticus 4 describes one form of this process.

The Lord spoke to Moses again, advising him what to do in the case of a person who sins unintentionally. This section displays the redemptive nature of Yahweh. Each group is instructed by turns on how to bring a sin offering to the Lord when someone sins unintentionally. In addition, a powerful refrain is spoken after guidelines for each group: "and he will be forgiven" (4:20, 26, 31, 35).

Why does God make such a fuss over unintentional sin? The answer is not found in our traditional human way of thinking. We offer excuses for unintentional sins and feel that we ought not be punished and should be easily forgiven. "I didn't mean to." Instead, an apology, punishment or restitution, which we will discuss shortly, is in order.

The answer to the question of why sacrifice is necessary for unintentional sin is found in the nature of God, his sacred place, and his holy presence. Sin, regardless of whether committed maliciously or intentionally, nevertheless pollutes the sacred space, potentially harms someone, and defiles the dwelling of the Most High God.

Therefore, an unintentional sin requires restoring the good creative order that God established from the beginning at the creation.

Sin Offerings

Leviticus 4 details the third type of offering: sin offerings, which include interesting variations on the burnt offerings and well-being offerings. Another name for these is purification offerings, and this name more directly describes what it actually does ritually for the community: purifies the person or community.

First, if a Levite priest sins, he is to bring a bull to the Tent of Meeting and after slaughtering it, dip his finger in the blood and sprinkle it seven times before the Lord in front of the curtain of the sanctuary (4:6). The priest then pours out the remainder of the blood at the base of the altar of burnt offering that is at the entrance of the Tent of Meeting. The fat portions from near the liver and kidneys are to be burned as in the burnt offerings, but a second difference in the sin offering is that the hide, head, legs, entrails, and dung from the animal are to be taken outside the camp and burned in a ceremonially clean place, the ash heap.

The words of the Lord then turn to a similar procedure in the event that the whole congregation errs unintentionally and does something the Lord said not to do. The offender offers a bull and the elders lay their hands on the head of the bull then proceed with the same sacrifice ritual as when a priest sins unintentionally. A ruler who sins is commanded to bring a male goat without blemish as a sin offering if he sins unintentionally then is made aware of his sin.

Finally, an ordinary Israelite is to bring a female goat as a sin offering.

With each separate instance—the unintentional sin of the whole community, rulers, and ordinary Israelites—the graceful pledge, "and he will be forgiven" is repeated, but this is missing from the conclusion of the section about the priests (4:1-12), and I don't know why.

Restitution

My grandpa was one hundred percent cowboy. I know my dad has ridden a horse, but he'd finished that phase before my memory began. I was raised down pasture from my grandpa, Ross Taylor and my grandmother Grace. People in our neck of the woods called my grandparents Amazing Grace and Old Rugged Ross.

Since grandpa was full blood cowboy and my dad was about half, I grew up a quarter cowboy. My brother and I rode horses, fed and watered cows and took them to sale. We didn't go on long rides or wear cowboy hats or depend on our horses for livelihood, so we were semi-cowboys.

Years later, in my forties, I learned something I never knew. I'm Cherokee. I'd missed it somehow. Maybe it is because we don't really look Cherokee, and our blood line is thin. Grandma used to say if you took all the Cherokee blood out of us, we'd survive. In other words, I'm 1/256th Cherokee, making me less than .5 percent Cherokee, but the nation still accepts me because my great grandmother Anna Coates is on the Dawes Rolls.

My view of the world shifted when I learned more about my Cherokee ancestors, injustices done to indigenous peoples during the land grabs of the 1800s and early 1900s. Federal courts have concluded that because of atrocities committed against sovereign people like the Cherokees, the United States government must pay reparations to many of these nations. Land reservations, granting of sovereignty and exemption from certain legal restrictions are some of the results that we see at work even today.

In the United States the popular legal term for these payments is "reparations." The same term has been used in the context of slavery, where descendants of slaves are later compensated by families, businesses that unjustly removed African Americans from land or deprived them of compensation.

A police officer once told me restitution is also an important idea in law enforcement today in many communities. Another form of reparations, restitution is the act of making right something that was wrong. For example, a payment might be made to amend for harm done to another person or property. Punitive damages are assessed in excess of the victim's loss to make an example to society for the cause of justice. Offenders must fear that they will pay for their actions, often in excess of the damage they have done.

Punitive damages not only discourages the offender from doing it again but also sends a signal to witnesses to curb any desires of doing the same thing. I recently heard, however, that in civil cases, there is no sure system in place for collecting those damages. A court may assess damages in a civil case, but they are not in the business of collecting it. The victim has a legal right to invoice and collect but must take further legal action if the offender does not pay up. Often a victim is a victim again of injustice, indignity, and neglect when a civil court ruling is ignored.

Our world is not so far from the world of Leviticus, is it? Some of the same legal actions still take place. Humans are still involved. People are offended. People are victimized. Justice is attempted or badly missing. In the world of Leviticus, when someone is convicted of defrauding someone or stealing money, a surcharge of twenty percent would be added as damages to the person offended (6:5).

The idea of reparations is as ancient as Leviticus. The idea came from God and the English word that gets translated in this context of life in Israel is restitution.

Exodus first mentions the idea of restitution (Ex 22:3), but the idea is developed in Leviticus 5 and 6.

Here the sin offering and occasions that put guilt on a person, even if unintentional, are expanded from chapter 4. There seems to be a distinction, however, between the sin offering for the intentional act, and the guilt offering for the unintentional act. The result of separation from God— intentional or not—is the bottom line, and restoration of that relationship is the goal.

Restoration

If you have ever testified against someone who has committed a crime, then you know how stressful and even fearful this can be. Though the desire for justice wells up in us, turning a blind eye to crime or an injustice is our human tendency when fear and stress comes to roost in our hearts. We may make an anonymous call to the police about a drug dealer in our neighborhood, but will we testify against him or her in court when called upon? Prosecutors face this digression daily in the attempt to convict wrongdoers.

In the world of Leviticus, absolving oneself of responsibility for a crime witnessed is unacceptable (5:1). There is a concern in this section for courage to speak against injustice, the need for ritual cleanliness, and thoughtfulness in taking oaths rather than rashly committing property or services to people. Again, there is an ongoing sensitivity to the poor, evidenced by two exceptional gifts to the lamb or goat for the guilt offering (5:6, 7, 11).

The shame of guilt is wrongdoing against the Lord and the guilt offering is a way to restore that relationship between the offender and God through sacrifice, an offering of a lamb, goat, ram, dove, or grain.

Leviticus 6 and 7 review and nuance earlier chapters. Why the repetition? First, repetition was not such a vile thing in ancient literature as it sometimes is viewed today. Second, additional nuance is placed on the burnt, grain, fellowship, sin, and guilt offerings. For instance, emphasis is placed on treatment of neighbor in 6:1-7. He must make restitution.

After reading again through chapter 6-7, notice the five major offering categories and a sixth that is mentioned in afterthought, in the summary statement in 7:37: the ordination offering, which is specific for the beginning of one's life in the priesthood.

The most important point of the six offerings is that sin separates the community from God, and something must be done about it. Sin also separates people, and something must be done about it. In the tabernacle system of Israel, offerings were implemented in order to restore fellowship with God and one another. Sin is viewed not only as a moral failure but also as an offense against one another and ultimately against God.

There is a recurring theme of comfort to the offender. Read that again: the offender, not the offended. Pay back what you owe and add to it, make your offering, and you will be forgiven. The phrase is repeated several times in this section: "and he will be forgiven."

Reflecting

Read Leviticus 4-7 then reflect with others on the following:

1. What do you *like* about the story?
2. What do you *not like* about story?
3. What do you think the story is saying to the *original audience*?
4. What is the story saying to us *today*?
5. What is the story calling us to *believe*?
6. What is the story calling us to *do*?
7. With whom can you *share* this story this week?

Prayer

Lord, may we never let our stubborn pride and personal vendettas separate us from you or from one another. But we harbor offense in our hearts—not just moral failure but relational failure. Is there someone you want me to remember today? Someone I've wronged, perhaps by neglect? Someone I've dismissed as a human being this week? Have I sinned against you, Yahweh?

CHAPTER 4

What Happens When God Sends Holy Fire?

Holy Clothes

I HAVE THREE BROTHERS, AND I AM THE YOUNGEST. I ALSO rank lowest on the dressing scale. My two older brothers often generously give me hand-me-down clothes and shoes, even in my forties. Subtle attempts to improve my appearance.

The Christian church I grew up in does not dress in vestments of any kind. Preachers have always been expected to wear ties, and these days they don't even wear ties but many, including myself, dress informally in jeans and pull-over shirts. On a recent glance at two side by side online videos of successive weeks preaching at our church, I realized I'd worn the same shirt two weeks in a row, a wardrobe sin in rich America. In poorer nations, having one shirt and wearing it repeatedly is no wardrobe sin.

Scot McKnight, who I call one of my "Theologians in My Pocket," one of those folks I look to for wisdom in biblical and theological matters, wrote about the difference between ministers in "skinny jeans" and those in "dress slacks." McKnight says you can nearly predict a preacher's theology by what he wears. Skinny jeans guys weight their sermons with social justice. Guys in slacks and ties weight their sermons with personal salvation. The contrast and comparisons are interesting and funny, but you can read more in McKnight's book, *Kingdom Conspiracy.*

I have a few friends who are Methodist, Catholic, Anglican and wear the vestments of the Christian calendar. While I didn't grow up experiencing these vestments, I think I get this in the way that Martin Sheen on The West Wing told his staff about the importance of the office of the presidency. The reason he wanted to be called "Mr. President," even by his close staff, was not because he was a demagogue but because he respected the office and wanted others to respect the office as well.

In some ways, I think the vestments say something about God, not something about the person who wears them. The person is saying, "God is more important than my suit and tie, more than my cool clothes and tattoos. I'm submitting to the vestments of the Church."

Likewise, the vestments of the priests in the world of Leviticus were not simply for looks. Exodus 28:2 says these sacred garments will give Aaron and his sons "dignity and honor." Moses is the outfitter for this ultimate task of going before the Lord. He orders the following items of ordination brought to the Tent of Meeting: the garments, anointing oil, a bull for the sin offering, two rams—one for a burnt offering, another for an ordination offering, and a basket containing unleavened bread.

The vestments of Israel were a way for the Levites to remember God is the one who clothes them, further reminding themselves and those who see them, how God brought the twelve tribes of Israel out of Egypt.

Aaron and Sons Clothiers

Chapter 8 describes the ordination process the priests pass through before entering the Tent of Meeting, the special attire for service, and the unique way they are ritually prepared to enter. Throughout this chapter, the importance of divine command and human execution is repeated seven times (8:4, 9, 13, 17, 21, 29, 36). Moses is given the task of clothing (8:7) and anointing Aaron (8:10-12). Special clothing shows movement from ordinary to priestly status and Aaron's unique clothes show his high priest status.

First, Moses washes Aaron and his sons with water (8:6) as a way of purifying them to do rituals in God's service. The text doesn't specify whether the priests were immersed in water to bathe or whether water was poured on them. Moses likely used the bronze basin that was at the entrance of the Tent of Meeting (Ex 38:8) to ritually pour water on the heads and bodies of the men.

Moses then clothes Aaron (8:7; cf. Ex 28). Underwear first, likely cloth wrapped from waist to thighs were put on, then a tunic—an ankle-length long-sleeved dress—would be worn next to the skin.

Moses then put on Aaron a purple, scarlet and blue robe with gold embroidering and bells on the hem so they would be heard when Aaron entered the Holy of Holies, and would not die. Once again our cultural distance from the world of Leviticus prompts irrelevant questions: What's with the bells? Does Yahweh not like being snuck up on?

The ephod was a flat rectangular piece that was tied with its own cords then again secured with a sash around the waist. On top of this was tied from its four corners the breastplate that contained the urim and thummim.

What were the urim and thummin? Nobody today is sure, but they may have been pieces of wood or bone used to make decisions. The modern day equivalent is to use a coin, heads or tails, for making a fair random choice when two parties are involved and need what we would call a fair and random decision but those in the Levitical world would likely consider the will of God in the matter.

Knowing what we know, let's not make assumptions that wise discernment was replaced with random judgments. It wasn't as if priests were deciding the fate of someone who sinned by flipping a coin: heads you get expelled from the community, tails you stay! Some scholars believe these words and their corresponding objects meant guilty and not guilty, but they could have been used as a deciding vote when an impasse had been reached in a matter.

Finally, Moses placed the turban on Aaron's head and a special medallion—the diadem or crown—on top of and pressed into the folds of the turban.

Putting It All Together

We now have in the world of Leviticus a sacred place: the tabernacle. We have sacred priests: Aaron, his sons, and the Levites. Finally we have sacred rituals to perform in the presence of and as a means of honoring and continuing the presence of God in the community of Israel. So these special garments indicate a sacred status of the priests to do God's commands in the Tabernacle.

While a privilege, standing in the presence of Holy God is fearful for Israel, just as it would be fearful for us. Moses issues a dire warning for Aaron and his sons to stay at the entrance of the Tent of Meeting for seven days as part of their ordination. Why? He tells them, "so you will not die; for that is what I have been commanded" (8:35, NIV).

During the ordination, Moses wipes blood on the right earlobe, thumb, and big toe of Aaron, and repeats this for Aaron's sons. This is another preparation for service to God in the tabernacle. They have been touched by and protected by the atoning blood, one more ritual that validates that they are set apart for priestly service.

As we reflect on the special garments prescribed for Aaron to wear, do we have a place in our experience to help you empathize with the importance of this new priestly status? We who commercialize and trivialize and fash-ion-ize clothing—can we know the power and significance of being clothed in sacred vestments?

Consider the importance of clothing and anointing of Aaron and his sons as preparation for a holy vocation—and a dangerous one: going before the Lord God Almighty on behalf of the people, into God's presence. You'd want some special clothing, too.

Blazing Fire!

The Tabernacle is complete, instruction on the three major sacrifices has been given, a sacred band of brothers has been called. These brothers have been given special clothing and specific rituals of worship to perform. Now comes one of the climactic moments of Leviticus revealing the power and glory of Yahweh.

On the eighth day of their ordination, where the priests had stayed at the entrance to the Tent of Meeting, Moses called Aaron and his sons and the elders of Israel together. He told Aaron to bring a bull calf for his sin offering and a ram for a burnt offering, both without defect. Israelites were told to bring a male goat for the sin offering, a calf and a lamb—both a year old and without defect—for a burnt offering, an ox and a ram for a fellowship offering, and grain and oil for a grain offering.

They were to do all this for one reason: "For today the Lord will appear to you" (9:4).

Sacrifices functioned to purify and sanctify a place for God to dwell. This is one of the most common misunderstandings of sacrifices among Christians.

Many American Christians, for example, would say the one-dimensional purpose of sacrifices was to remove an individual's sin. This is one purpose and certainly a central one—to purify and cleanse the priesthood, the congregation of Israel, and individuals—but these sacrifices were a means to the goal of God dwelling among them. The recurring phrases in Leviticus make clear that Israel is to seek this holiness because God wants to dwell in their midst and these sacrifices will pave the way for that to happen. So the goal of the entire program of sacrifices is to make a place for Holy God to dwell in fellowship with his people and to bring the community together in fellowship with one another.

Chapter 9 is the narrated form of the instructions that have led up to this point in Leviticus. What we miss when we skim over parts we think are repetitive, is the movement of the story from divine message to messenger—God to Moses to Aaron and the Israelites—giving instruction to obedience and enactment. Chapters 8 and 9 show this obedience and enactment of Israel's new ritual program for worship before the Lord.

So here we see in one chapter the enactment of the three major sacrifices.

First they offered the sin offering for atonement (purifying) and expiating (removing) sin (Lev 9:8-11)—a bull for the Levites. Next, they burned a ram whole on the altar as dedication—the burnt offering—to the Lord from the Levites (9:12-14). After completing the sin and burnt offerings for the priests, Aaron brought the offering that was for the entire congregation: the ram for Israel's sin offering, the calf and lamb for the congregation's burnt offering and added the grain offering with it (9:15-20). (See also John Mark Hicks, *Come to the Table*, Leafwood Publishers, 2008).

Finally, Aaron and his sons slaughtered the ox and ram as the fellowship offering—fat portions were burned on the altar and blood was sprinkled on the sides of the altar; Aaron waved the breast and right thigh as a wave offering before the Lord then kept that portion for him and his sons to eat (9:21-22).

So the fat portions of the fellowship offering were the Lord's portion, the thigh and breast the priests portion, and the rest of the animal was taken by the worshippers to eat. With the sin offering, only the priests eat a portion of the meat. The burnt offering is burned whole and no part is eaten.

With the fellowship offering, portions are given to the Lord, priests, and worshippers. If this voluntary offering involves a bull, the meat left after the offal is burned and the priests take their portion of thigh and breast, would still be hundreds of pounds and could feed hundreds of Israelite families.

A most incredible scene comes next.

After the meticulous preparation of the tabernacle and vestments of the priests and offerings, the Lord rewards their obedience and diligence and desire for God's presence. The reward is to show his presence in fire descending from heaven, an incredible show of his power.

Here is how *The Message* paraphrase describes it: "Aaron lifted his hands over the people and blessed them. Having completed the rituals of the Absolution-Offering, the Whole-Burnt-Offering, and the Peace-Offering, he came down from the Altar. Moses and Aaron entered the Tent of Meeting. When they came out they blessed the people and the Glory of God appeared to all the people. Fire blazed out from God and consumed the Whole Burnt Offering and the fat pieces on the Altar. When all the people saw it happen they cheered loudly and then fell down, bowing in reverence" (Leviticus 9:22-24).

The Tabernacle has been set up, the major sacrifices have been prescribed, and now Aaron and his sons and Levites are ordained as priests. A unique and ceremonially appropriate place for Holy God to dwell has been established, a chosen nation and chosen priests are listening for God's instructions, special dress for the priests is fabricated, and the suspense and tension is mounting for the coming presence of the Lord in the Tent of Meeting.

The event of God's appearing was exponentially important for the life of this new community. God was—the fire proved—indeed with them.

Reflecting

Read Leviticus 8-9 then reflect with others on the following:

1. What do you *like* about the story?
2. What do you *not like* about story?
3. What do you think the story is saying to the *original audience*?
4. What is the story saying to us *today*?
5. What is the story calling us to *believe*?
6. What is the story calling us to *do*?
7. With whom can you *share* this story this week?

Prayer

Charles Wesley was an English leader of the Methodist movement in the 1700s. He wrote a nearly unbelievable number of hymns. Are you ready for this? Six thousand hymns.

Of those six thousand hymns, only 1 in 400 covered texts from Leviticus, but he did write from sixteen texts in Leviticus. One of those sixteen texts is Leviticus 8:35, and the title is, "A Charge to Keep I Have." He received the idea for the song while reading Matthew Henry's Commentary on Leviticus, where the note for 8:35 says, "We shall everyone of us have a charge to keep, an eternal God to glorify, an immortal soul to provide for, one generation to serve." The hymn is printed in Charles Wesley's 1762 hymnal. (Graham McKay, *A Hymn a Day,* O'More Publishing, 2003).

Lord, in the words of that great song, "A Charge to Keep I Have," so also I pray to you for myself, my loved ones, my neighbors, my church (or synagogue, mosque, or temple): "We shall everyone of us have a charge to keep, an eternal God to glorify, an immortal soul to provide for, one generation to serve."

CHAPTER 5

What Would You Do If God Struck Your Two Sons Dead?

The Story of Aaron and His Sons Nadab and Abihu

AARON WAS A "PREACHER." REMEMBER, HE WAS THE ONE God chose to be Moses' mouthpiece in Egypt. He had a gift for words. He spoke words of blessing on Israel, he told their story, he was the priest who mediated between the sin of Israel and their Holy God who would dwell only in a people made holy by the cleansing and purging rituals of the Tabernacle system.

But after what happened very soon after the ordination, Aaron the talker was stunned into silence.

53

They had just built the Tabernacle, ordained the priests, enacted the first sacrifices and saw the terrible power and presence of their Holy God appear before their eyes. Perhaps when Moses saw the people prostrate themselves, the Levites with them, he had thought the people had seen the light, that there would be no more profaning the God of Abraham, Isaac, and Jacob with golden calf or goat idols. Now perhaps he was thinking they could move forward to the Promised Land and receive the full blessing of the Lord.

But more conflict was ahead.

It was during the time of the inauguration of the Tabernacle, after all the sacrifices had been made and the fire of God blazed from heaven and Israel fell on their faces before the Lord. Then the Levites ate the sin offerings, and along with Israel, they all ate from the fellowship offerings.

And they drank.

Nadab and Abihu must have imbibed mightily as they feasted on meat and drank a fermented drink of some kind. In context of the ordination and reference to not drinking too much wine directly after the episode (10:8-9), speaks volumes for this possibility that they were indeed drunk and disregarding the importance of God's presence.

In their drunken stupor the two sons of Aaron took "strange" fire (translated also as unholy, unauthorized; cf. Ex. 30:9), added incense, then each took a bronze pan full of the smoking incense into the holy place, inside the tent. They were acting on their own, drunk, disobedient, and going before the presence of the Lord with reckless disregard for the proper position of obedience and humility before the Lord.

And God judged their wicked hearts. Lightning or fire crashed down on them and consumed them, burned them to death.

Aaron's sons had been dramatically killed by lightning (fire) from heaven and dragged dead outside of the camp. Moses comments in the text directly after this, on this very different consuming fire of the Lord: This is what the Lord meant when he said, "Through those who are near me I will show myself holy, and before all the people I will be glorified."

Now Aaron—the "preacher," the father of these two young men and Moses' brother who had long spoken for him—was speechless.

Aaron was distraught. There would be no funeral. No dedication of their lives, their souls to God before burial. No recounting of how Nadab and Abihu with Moses, Aaron and seventy elders of Israel reveled in the presence of God, eating and drinking together in fellowship with the Lord (Ex 24:9-11).

Instead they were dragged out of the camp by their cousins. Leviticus 10:4-6 describes the scene, here quoted from *The Message:*

Moses called for Mishael and Elzaphan, sons of Uzziel, Aaron's uncle. He said, "Come. Carry your dead cousins

*outside the camp, away from the Sanctuary." They came
and carried their dead cousins away, outside the camp, just
as Moses had directed.*

*Moses then said to Aaron and his remaining sons,
Eleazar and Ithamar, "No mourning rituals for you—
unkempt hair, torn clothes—or you'll also die and God will
be angry with the whole congregation. Your relatives—all
the People of Israel, in fact—will do the mourning over those
God has destroyed by fire.*

In place of the funeral, Moses instructed the Levites
to take the remaining fellowship and sin offerings and eat
the meat at the entrance of the Tent of Meeting. Yet Aaron
did in fact mourn in his own way. He was deeply troubled,
silenced, dismayed over the tragic second fire storm that
burned his sons to death. Aaron did not feel like eating
and drinking, even the meat that was prescribed for the
priest to eat.

Along with the instruction to finish the ordination meal,
Moses gave important guidelines about the priests learning
to distinguish between the clean and unclean, the sacred
and the profane. This was important to Israel because it has
been handed down by God from the very creative order
of things—for instance, instructions from the beginning
about what humankind could eat and not eat.

In particular, the unclean of this passage and the particular context of the Nadab and Abihu story, is the sin
of disregarding the Lord's commands in the heart of man

and taking God's work lightly by entering the entrance of the Tent of Meeting drunk and ignoring the commands of the Lord.

Here is one of the few recorded times God speaks directly to Aaron rather than through Moses, recorded in 10:8-10 (NIV): "Then the Lord said to Aaron, 'You and your sons are not to drink wine or other fermented drink whenever you go into the Tent of Meeting, or you will die. This is a lasting ordinance for the generations to come. You must distinguish between the holy and the common, between the unclean and the clean, and you must teach the Israelites all the decrees the Lord has given them through Moses.'"

Fury of Moses Rises and Subsides

Moses was furious at this immediate detour from God's commands. He was angry with Eleazar and Ithamar, Aaron's remaining sons because he had learned that the goat of the sin offering had been completely burned up—like a burnt offering—and Aaron and his remaining sons had not eaten the portion of the sin offering as commanded (10:16-20). When the Lord speaks, we obey! Moses may have wondered if all of Aaron and his family were going to seed before the whole venture even left the ground.

First, Nadab and Abihu strayed and were swiftly made a chilling example of God's wrath on those who rebelliously disobey. Now, Aaron himself and his sons were breaking another law! Aaron was to eat the sin offering, but he had refused. Moses confronted him about his disregard for the command of the Lord (10:17-18): "Why did you not eat the sin offering in the sacred area? For it is most holy, and God has given it to you that you may remove the guilt of the congregation, to make atonement on their behalf before the Lord. Its blood was not brought into the inner part of the sanctuary. You should certainly have eaten it in the sanctuary, as I commanded," Moses said.

Then Aaron, sullen and grieving, replied to Moses: "See, today they offered their sin offering and their burnt offerings before the Lord; and yet such things as these have befallen me! If I had eaten the sin offering today, would it have been agreeable to the Lord?"

When Moses heard this, he was satisfied (10:20).

This is one of the most poignant, sad conversations recorded in the Bible between two great men of faith. We often overlook it, but what about the dilemma of the fathers of faith, seeing the text through them and through the eyes of God who will not allow his presence to be defiled?

The importance of the narrative in Leviticus 10 is not as much about what we learn about Nadab and Abihu—though certainly this is an important event—but what we discover about the nature of God. Is he the butler at our beck and call that we often want him to be? Do we have a problem with a God who strikes someone dead?

God has done this in other biblical episodes: a sinful generation was destroyed in the great flood, and only Noah and his family were saved (Genesis 6), Lot's wife was turned to a pillar of salt for turning her face back toward sinful Sodom (Genesis 19:26), Ananias and Sapphira were struck dead for lying to church leaders (Acts 5:1-11).

In each case, what was the sin of the people God struck down? How do we receive these stories today? With fear and trembling? In your experience, how has this story of Nadab and Abihu been applied?

In my experience, this passage has been applied to worship in the New Testament church. Nadab and Abihu are held up as examples of what happens when we mess up worship, when you innovate. In churches of Christ the passage has most often in the twentieth century been applied to instrumental music. The reasoning goes that if we, like Nadab and Abihu, bring "strange fire" of instruments in worship, God will be displeased, and in extremely radical teaching some even believe they will be in danger of death or hell if they stray from a cappella singing.

In my opinion, the story of Nadab and Abihu is not, however, about instrumental music, nor their lack of ritual perfectionism. Instead, God judged their hearts as no human can do and determined they had made a mockery of the rituals and laws by entering his presence drunk with fire that was not from the sacred altar. God speaks the point of this story in verse 3: "I will show myself holy."

A final point ought to be made that Aaron also broke the law handed down by Moses. He and his sons did not eat the meat of the offering as they were commanded. Why didn't God also strike them down? If this story is about ritual perfection, then we would expect Aaron and two more sons to be struck by the fire of the Lord. But that doesn't happen. Aaron is unable to stomach the food of the sacrifice after his sons are killed, and Moses calls him out. But when Aaron justifies his actions by saying, in effect, "How can I be expected to eat at a time like this?" then Moses is satisfied.

And we can be satisfied that this story is more than just a way to bend our modern day religious goals to fit our needs. The few stories of people being struck dead must be handled sacredly and cautiously, not to lose sight of God. God was, is, and will always show himself holy. That's the point. Can we reconcile this view of God to our view?

Reflecting

Read Leviticus 10 then reflect with others on the following:

1. What do you *like* about the story?
2. What do you *not like* about story?
3. What do you think the story is saying to the *original audience*?
4. What is the story saying to us *today*?
5. What is the story calling us to *believe*?
6. What is the story calling us to *do*?
7. With whom can you *share* this story this week?

Prayer

Holy Father, we fear you. We fear to be prideful or arrogant in your presence, drunk physically or spiritually on worldly pleasures and ignoring your greatness and presence. We dare not play with fire. Let nothing stand in the way between us—Almighty God—and you.

CHAPTER 6

Are You Holy Enough?

Practical Health

IN TWENTY-FIRST CENTURY UNITED STATES, FEW ARE tempted to eat a bald eagle or rock badger. We just don't crave the flesh of an eagle like we do a turkey or a chicken, and we'd rather not spend the jail time for killing an endangered species. As crazy as this seems, perhaps some of these distinctions find their source in the next section of Leviticus.

One of the most common explanations for the dietary and hygiene laws in Leviticus, laid out in chapters 11-15, is that they promote good health. This, however, is not the reason given in Leviticus. Leviticus says the reason for these dietary and hygiene guidelines is because God is holy, and they are to follow these laws to be holy like God (Leviticus 11:44-45): "I am the Lord your God; consecrate yourselves and be holy, because I am holy. Do not make yourselves unclean by any creature that moves about on the ground. I am the Lord who brought you up out of Egypt to be your God; therefore be holy, because I am holy."

So the story is tied to the table in Israel. I am holy. You be holy. Eat sacred food fit for God's table and thus humanity's table, so you can be holy. Discern what is clean and unclean so you can walk with your God and be his holy people.

Jews have been, for the most part, content to call these laws "chukim" (shoe-keem), or mandatory laws, which must be followed regardless of the sense they make. But as the *Jewish Book of Why?* points out, the propensity to question remains. Why does God care what humans eat?

Seeking meaningful explanations, some Jewish and Christian scholars have come up with interesting possibilities to justify continuing "kosher" food practices. Maimonides concluded these were to "train us to master our appetites; to accustom us to restrain our desires; and to avoid considering the pleasure of eating and drinking as the goal of man's existence." (quoted in *Jewish Book of Why?*, 85)

Some Rabbis have believed that separatism is the key to Israel's survival, that holiness means primarily being a people set apart. The logic works like this: an observant Jew may not even eat with a Gentile and remain clean, and if they cannot eat together, sons will not marry Canaanite daughters, and Israel will remain.

The larger context outside the world of Leviticus is that a strong cord relating to dividing clean and unclean runs through Scripture. For example, in Genesis, God divides night from day, heaven from earth. Clean and unclean animals were divided for Noah's ark. Levites were ordained to maintain the separation between clean and unclean. Jesus' parables hit the theme of dividing between clean and unclean in ways the Jews hadn't considered before: wash the inside not just the outside of the cup. Cleanse your hearts not just your ritually washed hands.

The rationale for these laws must not necessarily be practical, though they may be. While recent evidence in science shows these ancients laws to be prescient way before their time, that's not the point.

These things were part of the created order, part of the nature of Holy God empowering his people to walk with him and be his people. And he would be their God. They were to keep the unclean separated from the clean because God designated certain foods and animals and practices to be those of the Israelites, to set them apart for God.

Make the Connection Between Holiness and Life

In the next five chapters (11-15), Levites are called to a strong connection between holiness and life. In order to reflect God's holiness and image, they are to maintain this balance and distinction between life and death, health and sickness, clean and unclean. Holiness and the space for God to be present were disrupted by the lack of distinction of these life issues. The Levites were to guard what was sacred so that God could be present with them. There is a strong relationship between the altar of the Lord and the table of man.

There was something about animals, such as cows, that chew the cud and had split hooves that made them more desirable to God and his people for food. If the animal chews the cud yet does not have split hooves, such as camels, that is not enough to make the cut for clean consumption. These instructions were given to Moses and Aaron and the Lord gives several examples, including the one most commonly known—the pig, that has a split hoof but does not chew the cud.

In the next section (11:9-12), sea life is divided between creatures with scales and fins and those without. Crustaceans, then, are to be avoided by Israel.

The section on flying creatures (11:13-23) sounds more like a list of endangered species. American Christians might avoid touching these, motivated by fear of arrest for breaking endangered species laws, more than dietary laws.

These are also not birds we are accustomed to eating, which may be handed down to us from generations of not eating these birds and increasing tradition of viewing them as wild and not domestic. There are no qualitative features of the birds to distinguish them, as with sea life and animals—so the list of birds to avoid may assume that other fowl, such as chickens, are acceptable. Though a few cultures in the world actually eat bats, these are on the list of detestable flying creatures, and most of us have no problem avoiding them.

Flying insects are stipulated by the number of legs—though many of us were taught in science class that an insect technically has six legs—and a few examples of edible four-legged creatures are grasshoppers, crickets, katydids, and locusts.

Dead unclean animals, carcasses, are to be avoided and the one who touches them is to be considered "tamei," or unclean, until evening. Even clean animals that die are considered then unclean and one who touches the carcass is unclean till evening and must wash his clothes.

Further listed crawling animals, ones we certainly seem to detest by nature are rats and lizards (11:29-30; 41-43). Even an item of clothing may be considered unclean if a gecko crawls on it. It can be cleansed with water, and there's a waiting period till evening. If a gecko or lizard falls into a clay pot, the pot was to be broken. Detestable to the Jews are any ground-bound animals, whether they walk on all fours or crawl on their bellies—perhaps a harkening back to the cursed serpent of Eden.

As final emphasis in the chapter, the overarching reason is given for not eating foods that are considered unclean by the Lord (11:44-45): "Make yourselves holy for I am holy.

Don't make yourselves ritually unclean by any creature that crawls on the ground. I am God who brought you up out of the land of Egypt. Be holy because I am holy."

All explanations, other than this one, are speculative. The dietary laws are required because this is how God's people remain ritually clean, holy as the Lord is holy. God's classic declaration, "I am God who brought you out of the land of Egypt" seems to fit the context of dividing and separating and consecrating for himself a people. The Lord brought his people out and showed them how to worship him, how to remain holy and pleasing to him, how to stay out of harm's way in places like Egypt. It doesn't have to make sense when the Lord says to Israel, "I AM." But the sense of the passage is clear and more justifiable than any other explanation: "Be holy because I am holy."

Women Giving Birth

In chapter 12, The Lord speaks to Moses the requirements for women who give birth. Because blood flows both during menstruation and through the placenta, a separation is required to show the division between life and death. A woman is to remain in solitude for a week after giving birth to a son and two weeks after giving birth to a daughter. On the eighth day, a boy is to be circumcised but the woman waits an additional thirty-three days to be purified by means of a year-old lamb, or in the case of one who cannot afford a lamb, a pair of doves or pigeons. The sacrifice is a sin offering and burnt offering to make atonement for the woman and presumably to consecrate her for life and care of the new child.

A comparison is made between this time of separation and the woman's menstrual period. In the flow of blood is life and death. Israel is instructed to avoid blood, not to consume it, and to enact ritual separation when one comes in contact with it. The division between life and death is important in the life of Israel. In blood is life but it also means death. As in the atonement, blood flows to redeem and give life, but a sacrifice and sprinkling of blood enacts it.

Chapter 13 begins to detail the regulations for and cleansing of infectious skin diseases, rashes, and household mold and mildew.

Again we go back in time to imagine no modern medicine and means of ridding rashes with over the counter ointments and creams or visits to the dermatologist. These chapters specifically often evoke from modern day readers the notion that God had a way of promoting health long before medical science.

While this may be true, it often obscures the vital separation between clean and unclean, the real issue being addressed. In order to keep the image of God and remain a holy people who live and walk in his shadow and image, they must obey these regulations to keep their bodies and homes pure. The more we emphasize this one pragmatic modern explanation, the more it may sidetrack us from the deeper theological understanding of why God does what He does.

When a rash appeared on the skin, Israelites were to show it to Aaron or one of his sons, the priests. Moses and Aaron are instructed on several kinds of skin problems: rashes, boils, burns, itching, leprosy, and infectious diseases. Yes Leviticus often sounds redundant, but read these chapters compared to many medical textbooks and find poetry and rhythm in place of bland prose! Read quickly, it feels more like singing, "There's a hole in my bucket, dear Liza" than something boring. It has a beautiful rhythm and drives toward the importance of Israelites keeping their skin intact and pure. Compare this to songs we teach children in our country and others to learn good hygiene.

The conclusion of each rhythmic portion is that priests may pronounce a person unclean and put them in a period of isolation, check them again after seven days, then pronounce them clean or put them back in isolation as the priest deems appropriate. A leprous person remains outside the camp and cries "Unclean! Unclean!" presumably when in the presence of someone who may not know that fact. Clothes may also serve as non-verbal clue for others that the person is suffering from a skin disease that may be thought communicable.

When an article of clothing or leather was contaminated with mildew, the priest was to deem it clean or unclean. After the article was washed and isolated for seven days, it was either pronounced clean by the priest. Or, if it was the same or worse, the article of clothing was burned. We get a sense again of the bottom line for Israel in the summary to the regulations on mildew in Leviticus 13:59 (*The Message*): "These are the instructions regarding a spot of serious fungus in clothing of wool or linen, woven or knitted material, or any article of leather, for pronouncing them clean or unclean."

Ritual Cleansing

Mold or mildew is a homeowner's scourge both then and now. Today mold is considered to cause allergies and asthma and is not welcomed in a home, and inspectors even warn buyers of homes when mold is present. Mold was not welcomed in ancient Israelite homes either. There's a curious wording in Leviticus 14:34, "When you enter the land of Canaan, which I am giving you as your possession, and I put a spreading mildew in a house in that land, the owner of the house must go and tell the priest, 'I have seen something that looks like mildew in my house.'"

By the phrase, "I put a spreading mildew in a house in that land" does the Lord mean he intends to uproot certain people? While we might anguish over the presence of mildew in our homes, would we ever consider that God put it there?

The priest examined the house with mildew and locks it without inhabitants for seven days. If the mildew remains, they were to scrape the walls and even tear out contaminated stones and re-plaster. If this doesn't work and the mildew comes back, the entire house—stones, timbers, plaster—were to be torn down and taken outside the camp to the "unclean place." A home cleansing ceremony similar to the skin cleansing ritual is detailed in Leviticus 14:49-53.

Rather than avoiding such passages or considering them "gross," consider the implications of this passage. First, Moses, Aaron, and the sons of Aaron—the Levites—were responsible for keeping the people of Israel ritually pure before the Lord in order for his presence to remain among them. The danger of contamination from the unclean is God withdrawing from them.

One way that we might identify most profoundly with the process of cleansing from infectious diseases is from our familiarity with David's exclamation in Psalm 51: "cleanse me with hyssop!" Hyssop is a small shrub normally about two feet tall with small white flowers in bunches and was used in Israel to apply blood to doorposts during the Exodus (Exodus 12:22) and to cleanse those dubbed unclean by the priest (Leviticus 14:4, 6, 49, 51-52). Moses used hyssop to sprinkle Israel with blood (Hebrews 9:19).

When a person has been banished outside the camp, the priest goes outside to the camp to check on him or her. This is a powerful reminder that though the person is "alone" outside the camp, they are not forgotten nor are they left unattended. A ceremony of cleansing for one who has healed is described in chapter 14.

Two birds are brought and one is killed over a bowl of fresh water in a clay pot. Hyssop, scarlet yarn, cedar wood, and a second live bird are all dipped in the pot and the priest sprinkles seven times the mixture of water and blood on the person to be cleansed. The priest then pronounces the person "clean!"

The person to be cleansed washes his or her clothes, shaves "all his hair" and bathes. In this way a person becomes ceremonially clean. The person can return to camp but must stay at the entrance of the family's tent for seven more days then repeat shaving the whole body, even eyebrows "and the rest of the hair" are mentioned, and he or she will be clean. On the eighth day the newly cleansed person is instructed to bring two male lambs, a ewe lamb, grain and oil as guilt and burnt offerings.

Along with an atoning sin offering and the sweet smelling aroma to the Lord of a burnt offering, the priests did something that mirrors their own ordination. They placed drops of blood on the earlobe and right thumb and big toe of the one being cleansed. Then they did the same with oil and finished by anointing them with oil on their heads, another act that mirrors the priestly ordination. The live bird is to be set free in "the open fields." Provision is again made for the poor, who could bring one—not three lambs—and two doves or pigeons.

Bodily Fluids

Bodily fluids are associated with life and death—blood was life, the shedding of it death or atonement. Semen and the life-sustaining blood in a woman's placenta is life. When a man's semen or a woman's blood came out of the body and was "wasted," this was considered a situation that demanded a separation between life and death, clean and unclean, as noted here in 15:31-33 (*The Message*): "You are responsible for keeping the People of Israel separate from that which makes them ritually unclean, lest they die in their unclean condition by defiling my Dwelling which is among them. These are the procedures to follow for a man with a discharge or an emission of semen that makes him unclean, and for a woman in her menstrual period—any man or woman with a discharge and also for a man who sleeps with a woman who is unclean."

Men's and women's concerns for remaining ritually clean are covered parallel to one another. First, either intentional or unintentional emissions of semen make the male unclean until evening. He must wash any clothes touched by semen, himself, and remain ceremonially unclean until evening. An unhealthy discharge, such as an infection, from the male's penis renders him unclean and in need of seven days of isolation, washing the body and clothes, and offerings in the tabernacle.

Parallel to the concern for male ritual purity is the concern for females to remain unclean during the time of their monthly period. The flow is life and death and subject to ritual guidelines. In later Jewish writings is mention of women being immersed in a ritual bath after their period is over.

Another summary reminder comes at the end of chapter 15 to give us a key for understanding the chapter specifically and Leviticus overall. Note that the summaries tell what precedes it but the introduction to each section is action, such as "The Lord spoke to Moses."

In order not to end this chapter on commentary about bodily fluids, here's a reminder about the whole book of Leviticus. Once again, the key to understanding Leviticus and to anything mentioned, whether about bodily fluids, mildew, monthly periods, is to remember God is seeking a people for Himself, to be holy as He is holy. "Consecrate yourselves and be holy, because I am the Lord your God. Keep my decrees and follow them. I am the Lord, who makes you holy."

Reflecting

Read Leviticus 11-15 then reflect with others on the following:

1. What do you *like* about the story?
2. What do you *not like* about story?
3. What do you think the story is saying to the *original audience*?
4. What is the story saying to us *today*?
5. What is the story calling us to *believe*?
6. What is the story calling us to *do*?
7. With whom can you *share* this story this week?

Prayer

Lord, we come before you in your presence in need of your incredible atoning love. Your great sacrifice of Jesus is the offering we bring because we know it is your work in Christ, not us, that saves us. Once you allowed us to find restoration in sacrifices of animals, part of your creation as we are. But Jesus—who was not created—was given up for us for an all-time sacrifice.

So we know we have done nothing—except to be guilty of sin and culpability for his death—to deserve or cause your action in Christ but we respond to your grace by appealing to this act of mercy with a conscience made clean by the shedding of his blood.

Like those who were considered "unclean," so we want to get washed! In the words of Peter, "The waters of baptism do that for you, not by washing away dirt from your skin but by presenting you through Jesus' resurrection before God with a clear conscience. Jesus has the last word on everything and everyone, from angels to armies. He's standing right alongside God, and what he says goes (1 Peter 3:21-22, *The Message*).

CHAPTER 7

Where Do We First Learn About Atonement?

Big Gift to Theology

I SAW A COFFEE MUG THAT READ, "DON'T CONFUSE YOUR google search with my theology degree." Biblical texts and theology are no easy concepts to fathom, and even scholars with those biblical degrees have difficulty fathoming the depths of concepts such as the atonement.

Atonement is the topic of Leviticus 16. The atonement is the most important contribution of Leviticus to our understanding of God, Israel, and our Christian faith.

Two major objectives of the atonement are ridding and cleansing. Sins that threatened to separate Israel from

God were expiated or removed and the community ritually cleansed in the atonement day ceremonies.

For example, Leviticus 16 is built around various uses of the Hebrew word "Kippur." This is where we get the modern use of "Yom Kippur," the Day of Atonement celebrated still in Jewish synagogues. The Day of Atonement was established in Leviticus as an annual ritual of cleansing and purging accumulated sins of the priesthood and Israel during the past year. So, the word Kippur, that can mean variously purging, cleansing, expiating, ransom, covering, atoning, appears repeatedly in Leviticus 16.

First, let's take a look at what happened, then we will dig more deeply into what atonement meant for Israel and for Christianity.

The atonement is the centerpiece of Leviticus and central to the life of Israel. Why? Because at the heart of the Tabernacle system is the concept of cleansing and purging as preparation for living in the presence of a holy God.

The day of Atonement is the annual way that Israel cleansed and purged ritual impurity and sin from the camp. The immediate mention of Nadab and Abihu in chapter 16 probably indicates that this is a prime example of the kind of ritual impurity—the touch of death and wrongdoing—that needed expiated from the community.

Again the question is, "How are we to live with a holy God? How is the community to address radical impurity in the holy place of Yahweh?"

God is holy so he will not dwell in the presence of sin such as rebellious actions of Nadab and Abihu, shedding blood of a neighbor, or stealing.

Leviticus 16 details how Aaron in particular, and later his sons and other Levite priests who become high priests, are to enter the most holy place each year to effect purification. This annual ceremony was to address the violation between divine and death.

Description of Atonement Ceremony

On the tenth day of the seventh month in the Jewish calendar (16:29), 10 Tishri (Sep/Oct), an annual atonement day was called for by God.

Aaron does not enter the most holy place any day he chooses but on this day only, because God was present there in a cloud over the atonement cover.

For this special day, Aaron was to bathe before putting on a special garment, a unique white linen tunic (long smock) with linen under garments and a linen turban. Four animals were brought to the Tabernacle courtyard: a bull, two goats, and a ram.

The bull is slaughtered for Aaron's own sins and that of his household. The blood is sprinkled over the mercy seat of the Ark of the Covenant. The ram is given for a whole or burnt offering. Aaron carries a special container of blood into the tent of meeting, past the curtain, into the holy of holies and into the presence of God. In one hand he carries a censer full of burning coals and two handfuls of fragrant incense. He puts the incense on the fire and the smoke conceals the atonement cover above the testimony so Aaron will not die. With his finger he sprinkles the bull's blood on the front of the ark, then seven times in front of it.

Aaron is then instructed to bring two goats, one as a sacrifice for sin and guilt and one as a symbol of sin leaving the camp, an offering to the wild region outside the community. This wild region is termed, Azazel. They cast lots over the two goats. One was for God and the other was for what we have come to call the scapegoat, which we will return to shortly.

Aaron takes the goat's blood and also sprinkles it on and in front of the atonement cover for the sins of the congregation. "In this way," says Leviticus 16:16, "he will make atonement for the most holy place because of the uncleanness and rebellion of the Israelites, whatever their sins have been." He does the same for the tent of meeting. Then he does the same for the altar in the courtyard, sprinkling blood in the courtyard, sprinkling blood seven times (16:18,19).

Notice here something you may not have before: Aaron is cleansing the tent of meeting and holy of holies so God can dwell there.

Scapegoat

My wife, infant daughter, and I spent six weeks with Mennonites in Florida in 1994. With our mostly city-raised mission teammates, we learned how to live a farming life-style. Can that be taught in six weeks?

We were preparing for mission work in Africa, so at least when living among Ugandan farmers, we'd look some-what less foolish. Back at the Mennonite training center, we learned how to care for goats. We checked their gums for anemia, gave them shots for worms, fed them, played with them. Then it came time to slaughter them.

For those wishing to skip a gory detail, you may skip the very next paragraph.

We were to put the goats to "sleep" by conking them on the head with a sledgehammer, then cut their throats. I was nervous. I'd never popped a goat or any animal on the head. I knew this was done millions of times in slaughterhouses to feed me and a hungry world, but I'd never personally done it. I raised the sledge, swung down toward the goat, and the goat moved. Momentum carried the sledge past the goat and to my own leg. I hit my own shin with the sledge-hammer. I should have quit but in pain, I swung again and knocked the goat out. I limped away, hurting but feeling happy I hadn't broken my own leg with the blow.

For the Day of Atonement, a man was chosen for the task of leading a goat out of the camp—ritually and symbolically carrying sin out and damning it to the darkness, the wild place. Now, taking a live goat out of the camp —that I could do!

First, Aaron lays both hands on the head of the live goat and confesses over it all the wickedness and rebellion of the Israelites and puts them on the goat's head (16:21). "The goat will carry on itself all their sins to a solitary place; and the man shall release it in the desert" (16:27).

This man who escorts the goat away is ritually unclean until he bathes and changes his clothes outside the camp, then he can re-enter.

The idea of a Scapegoat is still used in modern English. But the concept comes from the amazing world of Leviticus. Scapegoat comes from the Hebrew word Azazel. The exact meaning of the word in Hebrew, Azazel, that has been translated Scapegoat, has been debated for centuries, but here are some possibilities for its meaning:

First, when the word Az-azel is broken down into two parts it sounds like "a goat that escapes."

Second, some think it simply means, "the wilderness or fierce region."

Third, still others believe Azazel is the proper name for a demon of the wilderness. They believe the goat is an offering for this evil spirit to keep such spirits away from the camp of Israel.

Today, in modern Hebrew, the words **Lekh la-azazel** are equivalent to the English "go to hell" or "get lost." Certainly, whatever the precise meaning of the Hebrew word, Azazel, pictures the action of sending sin out of the camp and into the wilderness or down into hell. This object lesson for Israel ensured that God's favor and blessings would continue for the nation of Israel.

After the scapegoat has gone to Azazel, Aaron changes into his clothes described in Leviticus 9 and exits the tent to give a burnt offering for himself and the people (16:24,25).

Atonement vs. Appeasement

Atonement is not the same as appeasement. Appeasement implies manipulating a non-existent relationship between two parties in order to realize a self-interested goal. Through atonement, however, God himself graciously provides the means of ridding the sin barrier between Israel and himself. This is different from pagan religions that feared gods to the point of bringing offerings that placated or appeased them so they would not destroy the worshiper.

The God of the universe and of Israel does not need appeased. But in his merciful wisdom he provides a way for his people to restore the covenant relationship that is broken when members of the community put sin between them and their God.

He allows them to cleanse the place so he can continue to dwell with them there. The offering is one of grace to his people, not a demand for appeasement.

As Christians, we view atonement through the eyes of the New Testament writers who see Jesus as the atoning sacrifice, replacing bulls and goats. The blood of cleansing is not blood of animals but of the Son of God. Again, he is not placating his own Father or appeasing him as if God needs such action but is providing the sacrificial means of atoning for sin that separates us from God. In Jesus we have been cleansed as the dwelling of the Holy Spirit, just as the tabernacle or later the temple was cleansed for the presence of God to dwell.

Jesus seems to understand at least part of his own purpose in terms of atoning. "For even the Son of Man did not come to be served, but to serve and to give his life as a ransom for many" (Mark 10:45). The one big mistake that people often make is to boil atonement down to one form of atoning: penal substitution. Yes, Jesus died instead of us, but as N.T. Wright takes an entire book to point out, atonement is a much bigger concept than the courtroom metaphor of a judge taking the accused's place. Ransom is another metaphor. Scapegoat is another metaphor. There are many, many metaphors that help us understand more fully what God has done for us, to forgive our sins and allow us to dwell in His gracious and glorious presence.

Paul speaks of the atonement of Christ in Romans 3:25-26: "God presented him as a sacrifice of atonement, through faith in his blood. He did this to demonstrate his justice, because in his forbearance he had left the sins committed beforehand unpunished—he did it to demonstrate his justice at the present time, so as to be just and the one who justifies those who have faith in Jesus."

Read Hebrews 8-9 in light of Leviticus 16; compare and contrast these two readings. Hebrews 8-9 gives the most detailed re-appropriation of the meaning of atonement for Christians, and it helps us to connect Leviticus 16 and Hebrews 8-9 in order to gain a fuller understanding both of the Old Testament understanding of the concept of atonement and the whole reason for the annual event, and the new way we understand it through Christ.

Singer/Songwriter Michael Card is the best artist/theologian I know who can put the Bible story into words and song. Look up the song, "He Was Heard" by Michael Card on a music service and listen, or look up the lyrics online. Michael Card makes a strong tie to the life and death—the atonement—achieved by God through Jesus Christ and the foundation for this atonement in the life of priests in the world of Leviticus.

Reflecting

Read Leviticus 16 then reflect with others on the following:

1. What do you *like* about the story?
2. What do you *not like* about story?
3. What do you think the story is saying to the *original audience*?
4. What is the story saying to us *today*?
5. What is the story calling us to *believe*?
6. What is the story calling us to *do*?
7. With whom can you *share* this story this week?

Prayer

Jesus Christ, our brother, our mediator of the New Covenant, our redeemer and God who was crushed so we might live, we praise you and stand in awe of you. Father, we believe with all our hearts you acted through him to restore us to friendship with you, with Jesus, with the Holy Spirit. So, let us fix our eyes upon Him!

As the Hebrew writer says, "Let us fix our eyes on Jesus, the author and perfecter of our faith, who for the joy set before him endured the cross, scorning its shame, and sat down at the right hand of the throne of God (Hebrews 12:2).

May we consider Jesus, how he endured, so we may not lose heart (Hebrews 12:3).

CHAPTER 8

Where Did Jesus Get That Bit About Loving Neighbors?

Be Holy Because I Am Holy

WHEN MY WIFE, JILL, AND I WERE DATING IN COLLEGE, WE went with a group on a hayride. After the hayride, I wrote Jill a note. We were in love, and in pre-cell phone and internet days, we wrote actual letters and cards.

We were attending a Christian college in Arkansas and were in the same Bible class. In that Bible class we learned that the whole "love your neighbor" thing Jesus taught came from Leviticus. When Jesus said, "Love your neighbor as yourself," he was quoting from Leviticus 19:18!

This was a significant revelation to me, and I wanted to quote this Leviticus passage in my love note to Jill. I was in the student center finishing the note, and I didn't have my Bible, but I thought I remembered the scripture reference.

So I signed my name and wrote the reference, "Leviticus 18:19," sealed the note and mailed it to Jill.

Jill received the note, we continued in love and bliss, and then many months later Jill brought up my note in conversation as we walked along a campus sidewalk.

"You remember a note you wrote me one time after a hayride?"

"Sure, but we've written each other a lot of letters and cards. Why are you bringing that one up?"

"Well," she said with a grin, I want to show you something. "You wrote this verse, 'Leviticus 18:19' on my note when you signed it, and I know what you were trying to write—that scripture about loving our neighbor from Leviticus 19:18—but you transposed the verse numbers. Read this." She handed me her Bible, opened to Leviticus 18:19 that I had inadvertently referenced.

Here is what Leviticus 18:19 says: "You must not go near a woman to have sex with her during her monthly period."

I fell over, stunned! We laughed until we cried. Jill had been slightly embarrassed for me, enough that it took some time for her to point out my mistake. Ha! Funny, after three decades together, it now takes no time at all to point out my mistakes! Still, I'm blessed my then girlfriend stuck with me and eventually decided to marry me, even after such a gaffe!

Here in this section of Leviticus I was attempting to quote from, are two very different kinds of texts. Here we find the famous passage Jesus quotes: Leviticus 19:18, "Forget about the bad things that people do to you. You must not try to get even. Love your neighbor as you love yourself. I am Yahweh" (Leviticus 19:18, IEB). But the same section includes passages as intimate, sexual, and personal in nature as the one I referenced in the note to Jill!

From here on out, you may want to double check scripture references. Do you trust me now?

So this next section, Leviticus 17-24, has been commonly called the "Holiness Code" because of its recurring theme of holiness in the life of the community. It's called the holiness code because of a key verse in this section is Leviticus 20:7: "Consecrate yourselves and be holy, because I am the Lord your God. Keep my decrees and follow them. I am the Lord, who makes you holy." Leviticus 17-24 is the "How to" section on loving neighbor.

Everett Fox, in his translation and commentary (Everett Fox, *The Five Books of Moses*, 1983), says the "Holiness Code" is "a significant statement of ethical code of ancient Israel which continues to speak to contemporary problems. The holiness idea is expanded from places and objects to relationships.

Again, the operative question is, If God is holy among us, how ought we to relate one another? This is a universal question for all times and peoples, yet we are given an inside account in the Old Testament of God's instructions to Israel and clues to how they lived that out.

The primal instinct to be God-like, to image God, is encouraged in proper perspective, says Fox. The improper way is to disregard God and other humans.

There is a strong connection between holiness of God and right relationships in the community. Leviticus draws closely together the idea that God is holy with the importance of fair and just treatment of neighbors, foreigners, the poor and disabled.

"Do not curse the deaf or put a stumbling block in front of the blind, but fear your God. I am the Lord" (Leviticus 19:14).

So the commands in this section relate to how to be holy like God in everyday interactions, sexuality, farming, dealing with poor, disabled, and foreigners.

Ancient monastic orders have in some way directly or indirectly drawn from the well of these passages that offer God's holy presence to those who are in awe and obey him in all areas of life. These holy communities have based many of the "rules" of their monasteries on the Holiness Code.

Here is an important transition from God speaking to Moses then to Aaron and his sons and priests into a broader address to all of Israel.

God tells Moses to speak to Aaron and his sons "and all the children of Israel." An interesting emphasis is a repeated phrase, "any man, any man." (Hebrew for man is Ish) Any man, any man who slays an animal outside the camp and does not bring it as a proper offering is guilty and will be cut off from his people. The Lord commands Israel to bring sacrifices back from the open fields and pagan gods to the context of the tabernacle. Worship returns from maverick wilderness and individual wills to the community and the presence of God.

So in Leviticus 17 we find the importance of the community both in the expansion of the commands to all of Israel and in the necessity of sacrificing within the community and not outside the camp as renegades. Life is holy, so sacrifice would be done in a ritually holy way and not freelanced in open fields. Blood and animals are vital to life and in all cases dedicated to God, and taking life at any time should be done with care and concern.

God warns Israel that neither are they to be like the Egyptians, where—God reminds them—they used to live, nor are they to be like the Canaanites where "I am bringing you." In no uncertain terms, God tells them they are not to practice what those nations do. They are to obey God's laws carefully. Why? The answer is the hinge of the entire section: because "I am the Lord your God." Yahweh reminds Israel repeatedly about His own holiness as a model for them to follow.

Sexual Relations

I once knew a woman who went to jail for sexually abusing a neighbor girl. She was raised in a Christian home, but she had never read Leviticus. Her Christian parents never mentioned Leviticus to her, never read this section about perversions, many of which she decided to indulge in during her life before she did prison time.

When she was in prison, she read Leviticus and wondered aloud what life may have been like if she had just had a more clear separation in her mind about what was appropriate and inappropriate, or in the language of the world of Leviticus, "clean and unclean."

Beginning with the sexual act that creates another life, Israel is to be holy. Immediately following this introduction to separation from Egypt and Canaan and their ways, comes a litany of prohibitions about sexual perversions, starting with the general and becoming more and more specific and grotesque, including beastiality and giving children in prostitution and even sacrifice.

"Keep my decrees and laws, for the man who obeys them will live by them. I am the Lord" (18:5).

Interestingly, verse 6 ends with "I am the Lord." This says something about the nature of God. God cares about and gives parameters for sexual life. Sexual relations with a close relative is opposed to the nature of God (18:7-18).

The connection between the prohibitions and the practices of Egypt and Canaan is clear in 18:24-30: "Do not defile yourselves in any of these ways, because this is how the nations that I am going to drive out before you became defiled" (18:24). The land itself was defiled and with additional graphic language, verse 28 says the land will vomit you out if you practice these things. In another recurrent conditional statement, "such persons must be cut off from their people."

The recurrent "be holy because I am holy" is restated in 19:1 as an introduction to a restatement of what we traditionally call the Ten Commandments, an expanded and different form. Interestingly this form mentions Sabbath and respect for father and mother first then moves to mention idol worship, though this is not to say the list is necessarily in order of importance.

A seemingly out of place guideline for making peace offerings comes in 19:5-8, but in light of all of chapter 17, which commands Israel to bring sacrifices back from the open fields and pagan gods to the context of the tabernacle, we again see the tie between the peace and community and the sacred in this inclusion of the peace offering here.

Loving the Poor

I enjoy getting the window seat on airplanes. What you can see from the air is amazing! I love flying over mountains and seeing the sunlight and shadows form a better 3D movie than anything on the flight. I enjoy seeing snaking rivers, cities—locating the stadium or famous landmarks like the

Gateway Arch in St. Louis or Statue of Liberty in New York City. From above I also enjoy seeing the patchwork quilt patterns formed by farmland. The way irrigation systems work today, often crops grow in circles, because it's most efficient for sprinklers to roll in a circle around a fixed axis. This leaves the corners unused or less productive.

I am reminded of this aerial view of farmlands, because Leviticus 19:9 urges just the opposite of modern day irrigation circles and leaving the corners to dry up. Israel is encouraged not only to plant to the corners of their fields, but when the harvest time comes, they are instructed to leave the corners of the fields unpicked so the poor and foreigners among them can "glean" food there.

In the strange alien universe of Leviticus comes a dramatic new connection for Israel to make, unlike any other nation: worshiping the One Holy God is connected to how we love our neighbors, even if they are aliens. The whole issue in the United States and Europe about legal or illegal aliens is a moot point in Leviticus. People are not legal or illegal but are to be viewed as neighbors to love if they are living among us. "Do not oppress foreigners who live in your country. Treat them just as you would treat your own citizens. Love foreigners the same way you would love yourselves, because you were once foreigners in the land of Egypt. I am Yahweh, your God" (19:33-34).

Interesting that the concept of "gleaning" comes just before the prohibition of stealing. The command not to steal is simple: "Do not steal." But the idea of not giving to the poor is a way of stealing what is rightfully left to them.

Even the corners of the marketplaces, places of business, were no hiding place from the ways of Yahweh. "Be fair when you judge people. And, be fair when you measure and weigh things. Your baskets for weighting should be the correct size" (19:35-36). Marketeers were great, and still are, at tricks of the eye and sleight of hand with weights and measures of flour, grains, and oils in the marketplace. There is no place God does not call us to honesty, even when doing our taxes!

"Do not defraud your neighbor or rob him" (19:13) expands from the simple prohibition, "Do not steal." The concern is both for the person to remain honest and free from lust for other's possessions but also free from the guilt of mistreating or defrauding a neighbor. Very practical commands about paying wages fairly and in a timely way— the day the services are provided—continue this theme of concern for the neighbor and the poor laborer.

Leviticus 19:14 mentions the cruel idea of putting a stumbling block in front of a blind person. "Instead, you must revere your God," as if cruelty to people is a direct affront to God. But the idea of a stumbling stone is more than just a cruel joke on a blind person.

When I was a young boy, a woman went before our church to confess sins. Said she had been "a stumbling block to others." I never knew for a long time what that meant.

Many years later when teaching a Bible class in Nashville, Tennessee, I asked the class what "stumbling block" means.

One class member said our church had been a stumbling block in our treatment of outsiders, because rather than draw them to the Lord we've often repelled them with harsh exclusivism. Another disagreed, saying the context of this text ought to lead to our application. The context, he said, is a recounting of the law in terms of relationship and the distinction of Israel from the nations, and the nations had no regard for their neighbors or concern for them. Still further, a third person in the class, an elder of that church, said we ought to remember the mindset of the ancient world, that a person with a defect, blind or maimed or deaf, would be considered not blessed by God, even cursed. But God was giving them a radically new way to view neighbors and the poor among them.

A stumbling block is "any object that may cause someone's downfall, whether literal (19:14) or figurative . . ." (*Harper's Bible Dictionary*). Idolatry is a stumbling block in the hearts of people in Ezekiel (14:3f). In Isaiah the people stumble over God himself (Isaiah 8:14), and Simeon in Luke 2:34 says the child Jesus "is destined to cause the falling and rising of many in Israel." Paul, in Romans 9:32-33, compares unbelieving Israel to those who stumbled over the "stumbling stone" because they pursued religion of works instead of Christ by faith. Paul calls Christ crucified a stumbling block to Jews and foolishness to Greeks—in Greek the word is scandalon, an offense. He parallels this with the tendency of believers who find new freedom in Christ to flaunt this and therefore make others stumble (*Harper's Bible Dictionary*).

While concern for the poor is thematic throughout Leviticus, 19:15 provides an alternate view: don't show partiality to the poor or the rich but judge your neighbor fairly. Israel is warned about slander, again reinforcing the idea of fairness and love for neighbors. Yet the second part of Leviticus 19:16 is puzzling: what were Israelites doing to endanger their neighbors' lives that a prohibition not to do anything that endangers life would be necessary?

Child Sacrifice

The heart becomes the locus of the next two commands in Leviticus 19:17-18. The second oldest recorded sin is one of the most universal and continuously difficult to conquer and reconcile: the sin of bearing a grudge, hating, or seeking revenge. By the time of the Leviticus commands, the sin of Cain murdering his brother because of hatred, had not been eradicated. Indeed, even after Jesus walked the earth and came to save the whole world from sin, we still have the gift of choice, and many still choose to hate.

While we may view Jesus' teaching one of the heart and the Old Testament one of stone, this is not necessarily the case. God has always desired the hearts of his created humanity to be holy and pure, not full of hatred for fellow humans but filled with love.

Leviticus 19:17 says, "You must not hate your brother in your heart."

It is very important to notice here that the tag line, "I am the Lord" comes with many of these prohibitions. We may ask, Why did God make so many specific laws? Why the repetition? But we are asking the wrong questions. The question ought to be, What can we learn about the nature of God from these laws, from the examples given? There's something of the character and nature of God that we can glean from seeing his heart on matters relating to treatment of neighbors, the poor, sexual relations, and his desire for worship to be for him and not for Molech or other pagan gods.

Here consequences of unholy sexual relations and idol worship are laid down. Any person who gives his child to Molech—for perverse reasons ranging from prostitution to human sacrifice—"must be put to death." The people of the community are to exercise the punishment by stoning (20:2). The repeated phrase in such cases—"I will set my face against that man and I will cut him off from his people"—is God's separation of the unholy from himself and the community.

Even the ones who stand idly by and allow a member of the community to give children to Molech without repercussion, stand in judgment (20:4). The phrase, "close their eyes" illustrates how they might willfully neglect to punish the wicked. Even the use of mediums or spiritists is considered "prostituting themselves" (20:6).

Remember a key verse in this holiness code section comes here in chapter 20: "Consecrate yourselves and be holy, because I am the Lord you God. Keep my decrees and follow them. I am the Lord, who makes you holy" (20:7).

More of those actions opposite of this consecration, those things that deserve death in the eyes of God, follow. For instance, to him who curses his own father and mother, "his blood will be on his own head" (20:9). Both man and woman who commit adultery together are to "be put to death" (20:10).

Throughout the next eleven verses, punishments are spelled out for sexual sins that mirror those listed in Leviticus 18.

Be Cautious with Land Texts

We must be very careful with the use of texts like Leviticus when it comes to the possession of land. The idea of "manifest destiny"—that Christian white people were to inhabit the whole land that eventually became the United States, used to be promoted even in public schools as a great American idea. Our ancestors in the United States used texts about God's people possessing the land and the inhabitants being vomited out in order to pursue evil land grabbing that many Christians believed to be God-ordained.

Again we must remember the goal of Adoniah, the Lord, seems to be the formation of a completely distinct people from the nations around them. Humans to this day have not been able to get our minds off the land, even in debates about the modern nation of Israel. But the point God was making with land was really about God's sovereignty over all the earth. God brought Israel into the land of Canaan and drove out the former inhabitants who did the kind of evil prohibited in Leviticus.

"Keep all my decrees and laws and follow them, so that the land where I am bringing you to live may not vomit you out. You must not live according to the customs of the nations I am going to drive out before you."

Because they did all these things, I abhorred them. But I said to you, "You will possess their land; I will give it to you as an inheritance, a land flowing with milk and honey." I am the Lord your God, who has set you apart from the nations.

All these laws and decrees add up to one goal of God: to set his people apart from the nations in order to be holy to them and find holiness in them so that He may be their God and they might be His people. "You are holy to me because I, the Lord, am holy, and I have set you apart from the nations to be my own" (20:26).

In the repeated frame of the Lord speaking to Moses and asking him to relay the message to Aaron and his sons, Leviticus 21 begins with a concession to the priests from the earlier strictures about touching dead bodies. If a close relative in what we in the United States would call our "immediate" family (spouse, child, parent) dies, the priest may tend to the dead body for burial. Attention is specifically drawn to an unmarried woman who relies on the care of her brother—this exception seems to flow out of the nature of God's concern for the underdog, the one without advocate, and the brother priest is called to be her advocate in life and in death.

With those caveats, the priests are told to stay away from the work of preparing corpses for burial. They are reminded not to shave their beards or heads or cut their bodies, presumably practices of pagan priests. It was important to set themselves apart from cultural practices of Egypt and Canaan. The priests distinguish themselves because they are the ones who "present the offerings made to the Lord by fire, the food of their God (21:6, cf. 21:17, 22), they are to be holy." This holiness includes marrying women who have not been defiled by either prostitution or divorce. This implies that they did, in fact, marry but were guided only to marry certain women who would not portray to Israel or aliens among them any tendency toward the sexual, relational, or cultic practices of Canaan or Egypt.

While chapters 21-22 are addressed specifically to Moses and in turn Aaron and his sons, rather than all of Israel, it seems in 21:8 that a broader audience is addressed to speak of their perception of priests: "Consider [the priests] holy, because I am holy—I who make you holy" (21:8).

Much is expected of priests, yet Israel is called to strict morality and ritually clean living as well. A priest's daughter, however, is specifically mentioned as an example of one who would be punished severely if she defiled herself by becoming a prostitute. She would be burned in the fire, and the text does not say if she would be put to death by other means first. Seems the threat of such suffering and ending would have been an effective preventative to a priest's daughter straying into such practices.

Still, even more is expected of the High Priest. He is not allowed to tend to his own parents for anything that would make him unclean, because the oil of anointing and responsibility of appearing before the Lord is on his head and shoulders. He must not enter any place where corpses lay, nor remain unkempt or tear his clothes in anger or mourning. A further criterion for his wife beyond prostitution or divorce is mentioned: she must be a virgin. Priests could perhaps marry a widow but the High Priest is not to marry any previously married woman or one defiled by prostitution. The reason given is so he will not defile the offspring among his people.

The specific work of presenting food on the altar or going inside the Holy of Holies is not to be done by one who has a bodily defect, and several examples are named, including hunchbacked, crippled hand or foot, wounds, damaged testicles. Here, the hackles of our inclusive society and thinking raise. We wonder why God seems to exclude rather than include those who have not willfully sinned but have birth defects. The looming question for us could be, If God allowed them to be born this way, why does he then exclude them from his service?

But there is a larger question than simply who is included. God does not necessarily share our specific cultural values, nor do we measure Him by our values. We ought not to allow the fact that those excluded from this specific service have birth defects to miss the overarching point of the passage: that it is God who sanctifies and prepares his priesthood for service and those who come into his presence must represent his holiness and his image. This does not necessarily say the ones who are crippled do not in some way represent or cannot represent God's image but only that they are not called for the specific duty of approaching the altar or curtain of the Tabernacle. In fact, those with defects are included in the sharing and eating of "the most holy food of his God, as well as the holy food" (21:22-23).

The theme of treating the sacred with contempt is pervasive in Leviticus, and the priests and Israel must take pause before participating in any activity that presumes on the grace of God or takes his commands lightly. Guidelines for the food of a priest's table are laid out: no person outside the family is to eat of the holy contributions of food. Yet again the Lord makes provision for slaves and women. A slave bought by a priest can eat from his table. A daughter who marries and is either widowed or divorced and has no children to care for her and returns to her father's house, may eat from the sacred contributions of food.

I Repeat, Leviticus is Repetitive

Leviticus is repetitive. I repeat. Leviticus is repetitive, but we ought to be careful in our attempts to read productively and skip parts we think redundant. Why? Because in so doing we miss details that say something more about the nature of God and his attention to detail, attention to the outcast, attention to justice. For instance, the next section, 22:17-33, details more about the requirement of animal offerings being unblemished.

The sin of Cain—treating the Lord with contempt by getting rid of undesirable fruit of his labors under the guise of sacrifice—is to be avoided here. No Israelite gets credit for a vow or thank offering or sin offering by killing two birds with one stone—getting rid of an undesirable animal through offering it up to the Lord. This is unacceptable to the Lord. Makes me wonder if all that credit we give ourselves for giving away "unwanted clothing" to Goodwill is really all that special!

The command (23:21) to eat thank (peace or well-being) offerings the same day would necessitate in some cases inviting neighbors, slaves, anyone who might need protein. They are constantly reminded: "Keep my commands and follow them. I am the Lord. Do not profane my holy name. I must be acknowledged as holy by the Israelites. I am the

Lord, who makes you holy and who brought you out of Egypt to be your God" (22:31-33)

"Later other festivals celebrating God's work in Israel's history were added by the Jews. Hanukkah, the Feast of Dedication or Feast of Lights, is held the 25th of Kislev (Nov/Dec). This festival marks God's miraculous supply of purified oil to burn in the newly rededicated temple in the time of the Maccabees. Purim, which celebrates the salvation of the Jewish people through the intervention of Queen Esther, is held the 14th of Adar (Feb/Mar)" (L. Richard's *The Bible Reader's Companion*, Wheaton, Ill.: Victor Books, 1991).

In Leviticus 24, two striking elements of presence and fellowship with God are described here: continually burning lamps, and bread set before the Lord. The priests had the duty and privilege of tending to the lamps and replenishing the oil, and eating and replenishing the bread. The lamp stand had three branches shaped like almond flowers budding on each side, a middle pole, so there were seven branches in all that would hold lamps.

The Story of Shelomith

The most striking part of Leviticus 24 is the story of Shelomith. The stories in Leviticus are not happy redemption stories but cautionary tales, and this is important to a better understanding of Leviticus.

There was once a man named Dibri, a descendant of Dan, son of Jacob and Bilhah (Gen. 30:1-6). His daughter,

Shelomith, married an Egyptian, and we don't know whether Dibri was happy or sad about his daughter marrying outside the Israelite people. The Bible does not say. Because he was a foreigner, the Egyptian may have been a slave or even indebted to an Israelite.

One day the Egyptian and Shelomith had a son, and Shelomith was instructed to remain in solitude for seven days, a ritual time of separation from the clan that allowed her to be cleansed from impurity and return to the camp after giving birth.

Shelomith and her Egyptian husband were living in one of the most phenomenal times in history. Shelomith's people had escaped Egyptian oppression, and her husband had joined them in their wilderness journey back to the Promised Land, Canaan. But they were soon to witness the great passion of the Lord and his people for holiness and reverence of the name of the Lord, though perhaps not in a way we might expect—the way Shelomith and her Egyptian husband must have experienced the discipline and holiness of God through his people would make many of us gasp in shock, turn away in shame, avert our eyes.

Shelomith's son, half Egyptian and half Israelite, got into a fight with a full-blooded Israelite. Though we don't know how old they were, they are at least of age enough to have a vehement disagreement over something that would lead them to grave conflict and struggle—the two scuffled in the camp (24:10). We don't know what they clashed over.

One could imagine dozens of scenarios such as a squab-ble over property or land, an ethnic slur, a prideful power struggle between young men.

What happened next is also a mystery but we do know that words were spat out of Shelomith's son's mouth with ill intent toward the Israelite man and the God of Abraham, Isaac, and Jacob. Israel was careful for good reason with the name of God, even to the point that in the text (24:11) of the story, the euphemistic "the Name" is used to pro-nounce God. To add insult and curses and perhaps invoking another god in a heated battle witnessed by several in the community would have attracted the hounds of hell on such a person.

We don't know how the fight ended, what happened to the fully Israelite man, but Shelomith's son was restrained and put into custody until the community could clarify what should be done with the man who cursed The Name. God spoke directly to Moses and gave him this prescription:

"Take-out the insulter, outside the camp, let all those who heard (the curse) lean their hands on his head and let the entire community pelt him!" (24:14, Fox translation)

The next several verses are words the Lord tells Moses to speak to Israel as further application of the command to keep The Name holy. There is a dramatic and repeti-tious emphasis to the section, as in many near-poetic lines of Leviticus. What the community would have heard in

Leviticus 24:15-16 might sound dynamically equivalent to something like this in English:

> *Any man, any man that blasphemes his God He*
> *will be held responsible and be put to death, yes*
> *death! The assembly must throw stones at him,*
> *yes throw stones at him. Any man, yes any man*
> *foreigner or native-born, who curses the Name*
> *must be put to death, yes death.*

Further injunctions come next related to taking life for life. This is one of the sources of the infamous "eye for an eye" notions that Jesus refers to in the Sermon on the Mount (Matthew 5:38-42; cf. Exodus 21:24). It seems the intent of eye for an eye was not only to punish but also to encourage fairness, to prevent revenge and over-punishing someone for a crime. In other words, a fly should not be killed with a sledgehammer. But when a sledgehammer is needed, it is indeed invoked, as was the case with Shelomith's son, which is the tragic conclusion of Leviticus 24.

Moses spoke to the children of Israel, and they took the insulting man outside the camp, and pelted him with rocks. They did as the Name commanded.

While stoning Shelomith's son resolved one problem, it brings up many questions and problems for us. How do we revere the name of God? How do we discipline in our communities? What does it tell us about God, this severe punishment along the lines of Nadab's and Abihu's death?

Reflecting

Read Leviticus 17-24 then reflect with others on the following:

1. What do you *like* about the story?
2. What do you *not like* about story?
3. What do you think the story is saying to the *original audience*?
4. What is the story saying to us *today*?
5. What is the story calling us to *believe*?
6. What is the story calling us to *do*?
7. With whom can you *share* this story this week?

Prayer

Lord, may we hear these words and diligently study Scripture, and treat one another with respect in a way that honors you! "Consecrate yourselves and be holy, because I am the Lord your God. Keep my decrees and follow them. I am the Lord, who makes you holy" (Leviticus 20:7).

CHAPTER 9

What are Ways to Live a Life of Jubilee?

Principles of Jubilee

I AM THE PREACHER FOR A CHURCH THAT BEGAN NEARLY fifty years ago. For the majority of those years the church was in debt in the millions. Bank loans, unfulfilled pledges, and big ideas built one of the largest church auditoriums in the country at the time. Years passed and debt became an enemy of the church growing, not a friend. The decision was made to get out of debt. It would take another book this size to tell the amazing story properly.

My only point is this. We said we would give God glory if we got out of debt, to forever say it was not our efforts but

God helping us get "out of Egypt," go through the Red Sea of Debt. To God be the glory, because we were redeemed from debt and now live free as a church from debilitating debt.

Our church lived the whole idea of Jubilee in an amazing way. One of the most unique ideas in history came from the world of Leviticus: to forgive debts and return land to its owner every 50 years—the year of Jubilee. After nearly fifty years as a church, we are free.

Among the many themes in the world of Leviticus, Jubilee is one many indebted people could use!

The Lord again spoke to Moses and told him to pass this message on to the Israelites: when you enter the land I am giving you, the land itself must rest in the seventh year. So they were to leave the farm land fallow in that year, meaning they would not plant any crops in that season. The seventh year was not the only concern—the eighth year was, when no yield from the crops would come.

God knew they might ask, "What will we do in the seventh year if we do not plant and harvest our crops?" Miraculously, however, God would provide a bumper crop in the sixth year that would last three years, until the harvest of the ninth year comes in (25:18-22).

The year of Jubilee was marked off by seven Sabbatical cycles plus one year. So every fiftieth year, on the day of Atonement in that year, a special time of Jubilee would be celebrated in the land.

This is one of the most interesting ideas for those of us who were raised in a capitalistic society and cut our teeth on ownership as a Christian-approved value that is encouraged. Frankly, we're amazed that anything like this can happen. How can land just be handed back to the ancestral owners?

Consider that an individual may only experience two or possibly three Jubilees. While individuals may not have experienced Jubilee many times in their lives, it's really not a ritual that's about individuals. Instead, it's a communal event that recognizes that land does not belong to humans.

This is the salient point of the year of Jubilee: land belongs to God. So the celebration called for families, individuals to return to their tribal land (twelve tribes of Judah) and acknowledge that it was God who gave them the land, who gives all land, and no man can possess it permanently—it is, instead, at all times on loan from God.

Case in point of God's ownership and Israel's use of the land is the content of the sale of land to one another. If an Israelite bought or sold crops, what he was really buying, says Leviticus 25:16, is not land. The land is God's. No, he was buying a number of crops until the Jubilee. If you are buying land, you might think of it this way: You are investing in the right to receive a certain number of crops or years until Jubilee from a specific plot of land God has given your people.

An important point connected with the sale of the number of crops—land deals—is this exhortation: "Do not take advantage of each other, but fear your God. I am the Lord your God" (Leviticus 25:17). This exhortation develops the second principle that is built on the foundation of the first related to property—land is God's.

This second principle is this: don't cheat one another or kick people when they are down.

Do Not Cheat One Another

What does not cheating one another look like in Israelite life?

Four examples are given, the first in Leviticus 25:25-28: "If one of your countrymen becomes poor and sells some of his property, his nearest relative is to come and redeem what his countryman has sold. If, however, a man has no one to redeem it for him but he himself prospers and acquires sufficient means to redeem it, he is to determine the value for the years since he sold it and refund the balance to the man to whom he sold it and refund the balance to the man to whom he sold it; he can then go back to his own property. But if he does not acquire the means to repay him, what he sold will remain in the possession of the buyer until the Year of Jubilee. It will be returned in the Jubilee, and he can then go back to his property."

The second example given in Leviticus 25:35 exhorts Israel to treat the poor as one who is an alien among them who is in need, and they were not to extract any interest on this care for them: "If one of your countrymen becomes poor and is unable to support himself among you, help him as you would an alien or a temporary resident, so he can continue to live among you. Do not take interest of any kind from him, but fear your God, so that your countryman may continue to live among you. You must not lend him money at interest or sell him food at a profit. I am the Lord your God, who brought you out of Egypt to give you the land of Canaan and to be your God" (NIV).

A third example is given relates to the poor who have absolutely nothing of value, except themselves and out of desperation sell themselves as a slave. Immediately the idea is contradicted as implausible with each other. It is dismissed as a disgrace to hold a neighbor or fellow Israelite as a slave but rather could be viewed and treated as a hired worker. Leviticus 25:39-43 describes what this looks like: "If one of your countrymen becomes poor among you and sells himself to you, do not make him work as a slave. He is to be treated as a hired worker or a temporary resident among you; he is to work for you until the Year of Jubilee. Then he and his children are to be released, and he will go back to his own clan and to the property of his forefathers. Because the Israelites are my servants, whom I brought out of Egypt, they must not be sold as slaves. Do not rule over them ruthlessly, but fear your God."

Anything about slavery is difficult for us to discuss, because we abhor it altogether in the twenty-first century. Israel, however, was urged to treat slaves with justice and goodness, and slaves would typically be from neighboring nations (25:44).

Finally, a fourth example is given of reversal of fortunes, if an Israelite loses everything and sells himself or family members to an alien living among them who has become rich. Essentially, the alien must also abide by the Year of Jubilee and allow the Israelite and family members to be free in that year. The Israelite retains the right to be redeemed by his countryman after he has sold himself (25:47). He may also redeem himself if he prospers, and the price is the number of years from the time he sold himself until the next Jubilee. At the end of this section the second major concern of this chapter—proper treatment of one another—is repeated: "you must see to it that his owner does not rule over him ruthlessly (25:53).

Concluding Leviticus 25 is a third major concern for Israel related to property. The first is that all land is God's. The second is that they do not cheat one another and not treat one another ruthlessly in property dealings. The third and concluding concern is that Israel remember always that they are God's servants in the land. No alien is to permanently possess them. They are God's possession and servants. The year of Jubilee, then, is to enforce this concern of God's to preserve His for-all-time people. The exodus is invoked again as the overriding grace that compels them, not as forced unwilling servants but as grateful, humble servants who know how God saved them from slavery itself in Egypt. "They are my servants, whom I brought out of Egypt. I am the Lord your God" (25:55).

A second Michael Card song is a great illustration of this section on the Jubilee. Card's interpretation is that Jubilee is an allegory for Christ's wiping away our overwhelming, unpayable debt. Look up online or on your music service, "Jubilee" by Michael Card.

Reflecting

Read Leviticus 17-24 then reflect with others on the following:

1. What do you *like* about the story?
2. What do you *not like* about story?
3. What do you think the story is saying to the *original audience*?
4. What is the story saying to us *today*?
5. What is the story calling us to *believe*?
6. What is the story calling us to *do*?
7. With whom can you *share* this story this week?

Prayer

Lord, you provided for a time for the slaves to be set free, for debts to all be canceled, so Your chosen ones could see. Your deep desire is for forgiveness, you long to see our liberty. And your yearning is embodied in the year of Jubilee! At your appointed time, your deep desire became a man. In the voice of Jesus the Messiah we hear the Jubilee trumpet sound that tells us we are free. And your yearning is embodied, Lord, in Jesus Christ! Jesus is the Jubilee! Debts forgiven! Slaves set free. Jesus is our Jubilee!" (Adapted from Michael Card, "Jubilee!")

CHAPTER 10

Yahweh Loves Forever

God Keeps His Covenant Forever

LEVITICUS 26 REINFORCES HUMAN CAPACITY TO PARTIC-
ipate in the outcome of God blessing them. In other words,
they were not left to the whims of gods or of a God who
arbitrarily blessed or cursed but could be certain that if
they kept their end of the covenant, they would prosper
and be blessed.

Chapter 26 may have been the original ending. Some
who study ancient texts believe chapter 27 was added later.
One thing is certain: Leviticus 26 is similar to endings in
the ancient Near Eastern treaties. And though Leviticus is

no ordinary treaty, it is a life-or-death covenant with God. Blessings would flow from God if they kept the covenant, but curses and devastation would come on Israel if they broke covenant with Yahweh (see also Deuteronomy 28-30; Exodus 23:25-33; Joshua 24:20-21).

Throughout Leviticus the goal has been to explain to Israel what life in the presence of a holy God of the universe would be like. God chose to dwell with them in the tabernacle, to communicate through Moses and Aaron, to be pleased with aromas of their burnt offerings and incense, to pour out forgiveness just as they poured out atoning blood of goats and bulls. All this took place as a covenant with the one who redeemed Israel from slavery and committed to be their God. And they would be his people.

Compare the covenant with parenting. Experts tell us that giving children choices and consequences of those choices is good parenting. Though the parallel quickly breaks down, of course, the Lord models this good parenting pattern of choices or consequences. God's goal is keeping the covenant (26:45). No matter what happens to the Israelites, no matter how far into idolatry and evil they go, God will not break his part of the bargain.

God therefore is a covenant maker and keeper, and these last chapters of Leviticus serve to remind his people of the covenant that God made with them, his dramatic redemption of an entire nation from slavery, and his relentless pursuit of his people either to bless them and bring them rain when they take the proper place as his slaves turned obedient servants, or to bring punishment for their sins "seven times over" when they reject him.

Blessing

Several word patterns appear in this chapter and the words are vivid and motivational to Israel and for us. Here we see a shorter form of the commands and concerns of God such as forbidding idolatry and observing Sabbaths and honoring the presence of God in the tabernacle, and the focus is on the consequences.

First, the Lord lays out the consequences of right and holy living as described in the previous chapters of Leviticus; the if-then statement comes in Leviticus 26:3-4: "If you follow my decrees and are careful to obey my commands, [then] I will send you rain in its season, and the ground will yield its crops and the trees of the field their fruit."

The Lord continues to pour out promises of blessing in several areas: plentiful rain and crops (26:4-5,10), peace and security (26:6-8), favor of God (26:9), presence of God (26:11), walking among them and being their God (26:12), liberation from slavery (26:13), ability of Israel to walk with heads held high (26:13).

But blessing comes only with obedience. Is His love conditional? He does love and pursue and discipline uncon-ditionally. He has established a covenant with Israel that has not and will not fail. When Israel goes wrong, he pursues with chastening, punishment in order to bring them back.

We often speak of unconditional love. God's love is indeed unconditional, but another way to say it is that God's love is "steadfast" and His covenant has conditions for Israel to keep in order for Israel to receive the blessings of God.

Cursing

By breaking the covenant, Israel incurs the wrath of the holy God. The list of curses in the event of disobedience or breaking the covenant, is much longer than the blessing section. This, again, mirrors the pattern of treaties in the ancient Near East, which had long sections of punishments and shorter sections on blessing. Since the curses, or consequences, are much more extensive than the blessings, a list of them would be tedious and in the process we might miss the whole point: keeping the covenant through holy living.

The section on punishment for disobedience or spurning the covenant (26:14-39) is a six-fold warning against breaking the covenant. A seventh statement (26:40-46) is very important as God's reversal of the curse and return of blessing if Israel confesses their sins.

Each warning is unique but similar enough to raise the question about whether this section may have been used in the ritual worship of Israel as a chant or recurrent oral warning to Israel against disobedience. A few other examples of repeating phrases are "if you do not listen to me," "I will punish you seven times over," and "if in spite of these things you do not accept my correction but continue to be hostile toward me."

The objective of noticing such repeating phrases is the same objective we have returned to throughout Leviticus: to learn what concerns God and how he wants us to live the holy life he requires in his presence. God wants us to listen to him (26:14, 18, 21, 27), he wants to break down stubborn pride and hostility in his people (26:19, 21, 23). He doesn't expect perfection, because he gives opportunity for confession (26:40) and paying for sin (26:41).

The language of God's chastening Israel for breaking covenant is vivid. The sky like iron and unyielding bronze soil will be God's atmosphere for breaking stubborn pride. If that doesn't affect his people, he will continue with more punishments—reminiscent of the progressively worse plaques in Egypt. Wild animals will attack Israel and rob their children, "multiply your afflictions seven times over, as your sins deserve" (26:21). If Israel continues to spurn correction and continues to be hostile, God himself will show them what hostility really is: enemies will attack, they will withdraw into their cities for security but will be afflicted with sickness and given into enemy hands as starving, desperate people (26:23-26).

Then if in spite of this, Israel still did not repent, God's anger (26:28) would burn toward an unrepentant people and strike them with such a severe famine that Israel would cannibalize their own children (26:29). Meanwhile the high places would be destroyed and dead bodies would be piled on top of the heap of idols. Many would be scattered, exiled, and the land of Canaan would be laid waste so much that the nations would marvel at it. If any remained, they would cower so much that a windblown leaf would terrify them and send them screaming and running for their lives, even though no one is pursuing them. Any remaining people would waste away in the land of their enemies because of their sins and the sins of their fathers (26:36-39).

The section, however, does end with a note of hope. Confessing Israel's sins and the sins of the fathers will lead to God remembering his covenant with Abraham, Isaac, and Jacob (26:40-41). And God will not only remember the people but the land itself (26:42). In fact, there is a vital connection between the Israelite people and their land. Without them the land lay fallow and desolate (26:43), but despite this and the sins of the people, the Lord chooses to not completely destroy them as a sign of his covenant keeping. The statement, "I am the Lord their God" emphasizes the permanence of the covenant: God is the God who makes and keeps covenants.

The chapter ends with the reminder of God's redemption of Israel from slavery that was done in the sight of all the nations. The conclusion reminds the people that these laws were established at Mount Sinai as a way to maintain a holy relationship between God and Israel.

Vows

My life got better when I learned the mantra, "Under promise and over deliver!" The converse cautionary version was how I'd often lived: "Over promise and under deliver."

This last chapter of Leviticus, of course, is more serious than a business mantra. Lives and God's honor is at stake.

Though it seems Leviticus 27 may have been added later to the book, it is a good addendum to the keeping of the sacred space for God that focuses on the ongoing dedication of people, property, and animals to God through vows.

The major focus on vows in this text and others (see also Deuteronomy 23:21–23; Ecclesiastes 5:2–7; Proverbs 20:25) is not the requirement to make extra vows but the desire of God that if people do in their zeal make vows to the Lord, that they keep them.

Much is made in this chapter of the surcharge of twenty percent to be paid when someone dedicates a person in service of the priests and tabernacle, an animal, or property and then wants to get that person, animal, house, or piece of land back. So the major emphases are keeping vows and paying an additional fifth of the value if one wants to go back on that commitment. But there is also a concern for the priests to have limitations. In ancient Egypt and Mesopotamia, priests abused the privileges of land and sacrifices for their own gain. This was unacceptable to God.

The first section (27:1-8) concerns dedication of individuals to the service of God, the tabernacle, or the priests.

A good example of a vow of a person is Samuel. The story is moving and worth another reading and will go far in understanding Leviticus 27:1-8.

Hannah was harassed by her co-wife Peninnah because Peninnah had children and Hannah didn't. Though their husband, Elkanah, tried to comfort her, she rose in the presence of Eli by the doorpost of the Tabernacle and cried out "in bitterness of soul" (I Samuel 1:10), wept much and prayed to God. In her distress and zeal she made this vow: "O Lord Almighty, if you will only look upon your servant's misery and remember me, and not forget your servant but give her a son, then I will give him to the Lord for all the days of his life, and no razor will ever be used on his head" (I Samuel 1:11). Later in the story (I Samuel 1:19), the text says "the Lord remembered her" and Elkanah and Hannah conceived, she named him Samuel, which sounds like "heard of God." Then she dedicated Samuel to the service of Eli and the priests (I Samuel 1-3).

The next section (27:9-13) is singularly concerned with animals used for vows being ritually pure, an earlier issue in Leviticus related to sacrifices. No deception would be tolerated from a person attempting to dedicate an animal that is bad and wouldn't have been much use to the person in the first place. Perhaps a person could reason, this animal is second-rate, so I can both cull it from my herds and make a vow at the same time. An animal so dedicated could be redeemed if a person needed the animal back, but twenty percent was added to the value to get it back.

Houses and land (27:14-25) were also used for vows to the Lord, and as with animals, the priest judges its value. If the man who dedicated it wants it back, he would pay an additional twenty percent to the priest. This all strikes us in the twenty-first century as implausible, that a person could give up his house then ask for it back and be penalized twenty percent of its value, but the emphasis here is on keeping vows. If one makes a vow, the expectation is to keep it, thus the stiff penalty for one who goes back on a vow or dedication of service, animals, house, or land. In the case of land, redemption of property was subject to the cycle of Jubilee and values were set or pro-rated according to the number of years until Jubilee (27:16-25).

Here is an example of a dedication of a field, and it may adjust our understanding of what was happening in the early church to know that dedication of land was not unique to the new Christian zeal. Certainly those dedicating land were zealous for the new way of following Jesus the Christ, but they were acting in very Israelite ways in response: "Joseph, a Levite from Cyprus, whom the apostles called Barnabas (which means Son of Encouragement), sold a field he owned and brought the money and put it at the apostles' feet" (Acts 4:36,37).

Juxtaposed with that account of Barnabas is the chilling account of Ananias and Sapphira being struck down for their deception of trying to pass off a capital gain for themselves as a total dedication to the Lord (Acts 5:1-11).

The last section again presses the point that everything belongs to the Lord. This should not be missed in the intricate and sometimes difficult to understand details in this text, such as the phase, "No person devoted to destruction may be ransomed; he must be put to death." Phrases such as this are both hard to decipher and given a few options, none are very satisfying. This may refer to the practice of setting a person or property aside for divine use.

The logic of Leviticus 27 goes something like this, according to Jacob Milgram: proscriptions are "most sacred" and irredeemable. Offerable animals, be they firstborn, tithes, or consecrations, are also irredeemable, and non-offerable consecrations, such as impure animals, land, houses, and crops (except when they are proscriptions), are redeemable.

Indeed, God wants us to listen to him (26:14, 18, 21, 27), he wants to break down stubborn pride and hostility in his people (26:19, 21, 23). He doesn't expect perfection, because he gives opportunity for confession (26:40) and paying for sin (26:41).

Reflecting

Read Leviticus 25-27 then reflect with others on the following:

1. What do you *like* about the story?
2. What do you *not like* about story?
3. What do you think the story is saying to the *original audience*?
4. What is the story saying to us *today*?
5. What is the story calling us to *believe*?
6. What is the story calling us to *do*?
7. With whom can you *share* this story this week?

Prayer

Lord, no matter what happens to the Israelites, no matter what happens to us, regardless how far into idolatry and evil Israel goes, how far in idolatry and evil of our own, still you have kept your end of the bargain. You are a covenant maker and keeper, dramatically redeeming an entire nation from slavery, and still today you relentless pursue us either to bless us or to bring punishment for our sins "seven times over" when we reject you.

Lord, What Do You Want Me to Do?

MAYBE YOU SKIPPED TO THE CONCLUSION, OR YOU PLOD-
ded your way through the book, or you happened to drop
the book and it opened to this page. Whatever the case, I'm
honored you made it this far.

Even after all I've said, to our "modern" minds, we still
tend to think Leviticus is horribly out of touch and in fact
some of us just think it's horrible, period. I've tried to view
the book of Leviticus much differently. Have you caught a
glimpse of Leviticus for what it was to Israel? An account
of the amazing event of Holy God calling a people out of
Egypt and into a life of fellowship with Himself and others
in community.

I have a habit of adding to my books some new spiritual insight that God has shown me during the writing. Sometimes it seems the new insight is on another track from the writing, but when I reflect, it comes because the biblical book I'm writing about has given me a new way of seeing, and it makes me more spiritually aware in other areas of my life and relationships.

The spiritual insight I learned during the writing of this book comes from Heidi Baker, missionary in Mozambique. Featured in the documentary, "The Finger of God," Baker suggests the miracles she has prayed for and witnessed are really about the love of God being revealed in the world. She encourages the "western church" (generally American and European churches that have stagnated and don't believe in the miraculous power of God) to do one thing to show the love of God in one person's life each day.

I took this exhortation from Heidi Baker into my life, and each day I am trying to show the love of God specifically to one person who I believe God is leading me to. It isn't always easy, but I am seeing God bring those people into my path and the question becomes, "God, what do you want me to do?"

My hope is that this study has made you more aware that God is calling you, too. God continues to call people to Himself, for deeper relationship with him, with others in community. The calling is to love God so deeply that your one question continues daily to be, "Lord, what do you want me to do?"

Leviticus matters because it shows us how people did and didn't listen when God called. One of the operative questions of individualism and consumerism is "Why?" It works in business, technology, and even in spirituality to get us below the surface and to something better.

My children, like yours or ones you may know, made it a habit of asking six "whys" before breakfast. And sometimes the response to answering one of their why questions was one more "Why?"

Just as the parent becomes exhausted with the why questions, I wonder if God doesn't get exasperated at our endless whys. Why questions are important to ask, but why questions are also important to stop asking at some point.

The next question after we get through our whys is this: OK, God what do you want me to do? At some point the repeated why question becomes a smokescreen for doing nothing.

Leviticus matters because we watch the first batch of God's worshiping people doing what they are asked to do. That's a counterculture movement today: doing what someone else tells us to do. It's actually an important value in our world, but as Americans we're often adverse to others telling us what to do. Why? We cut our teeth on rugged and radical individualism, and we don't like anyone telling us we can or can't do something.

Yet everyday we live with laws, with parents, with spouses and bosses (sometimes that's one in the same) who tell us what to do, and it's necessary that we do what we're told. What's so wrong with doing what's asked of us? Russian-born comedian Yakov Smirnoff said his dad would often say, "Son, your mother and I have a marriage that works for one simple reason: I don't run your mother's life. And, I don't run my life."

The operative question for the world of Leviticus is not "Why?" The operative question in the world of Leviticus is, "What do you want me to do, Lord?" Interestingly, for some mystics, this is the same important operative question in order to not get stuck inside our own heads, trapped in our grief over the why of a death or something not going our way.

So if there's one thing out of Leviticus that I can leave with you, it's this one question. If all of Leviticus is important for us to learn to ask with all sincerity and submission, "What do you want me to do, Lord?" then this study has had eternal value of leading us one step closer to Yahweh of the world of Leviticus.

God is calling you. Are you ready to ask with all sincerity and humility, "Lord, what do you want me to do?"

Where Can I Find More on Leviticus?

Resources for Further Growth

THE GOAL OF STUDY IS TO COME CLOSER TO GOD. PEOPLE often call this Spiritual Growth. I have tried to include applications and prayers in each chapter that will help individuals and groups grow spiritually, closer to God, in this study.

A short Bible study guide like this one cannot cover all the complexities of a book such as Leviticus. I have assumed the received text (the one we have in most modern English translations) and commented on it. In other words, I have not broken it down, as many scholars do, into chunks they think were written by different sources at different times (called redaction criticism).

My study assumes Mosaic authorship in principle, but our faith ought not be shaken if we find inconsistencies in the text because for a text written in the thirteenth century B.C. Many people were involved in recording and handing down the oral traditions and written traditions of the Hebrew people.

If available at a library near you, here are some commentaries that may help you go deeper in study. While many free study tools are available online at *Biblegateway. com* and other Bible sites, good commentaries and study guides are not always available for free online. Dig deeper! I use Logos software, which also includes many good commentaries, but this costs money. Is God's word worth an investment to you? What other media do we spend money on regularly?

. . . .

Budd, Philip J. Leviticus, *New Century Bible Commentary*. Grand Rapids: New Century/Eerdmans, 1996.

Butterworth, Mike. *Leviticus*. The People's Commentary. Oxford, England: The Bible Reading Fellowship, 2003.

Fox, Everett. *The Five Books of Moses*. The Schocken Bible Vol. 1, A new translation with Introductions, Commentary, and notes by Everett Fox, Illustrations by Schwebel. New York: Schocken Books, 1995.

Hartley, John E. *Leviticus*. Word Biblical Commentary. Dallas: Word, 1992.

Milgram, Jacob. *Leviticus: a book of ritual and ethics*. A Continental Commentary. Minneapolis: Fortress Press, 2004.

Milgram, Jacob. *Leviticus* 1-16, 17-22, 23-27, A New Translation with Introduction and Commentary. New York: Doubleday, 1991, 2000, 2001.

Bailey, Lloyd. *Leviticus*, Knox Preaching Guides. Atlanta: John Knox Press, 1987.

Balentine, Samuel E. *Leviticus. Interpretation: A Bible Commentary for Teaching and Preaching*. Louisville: John Knox Press, 2002.

Grabbe, Lester L. *Leviticus. Old Testament Guides*. Sheffield, England: Sheffield Academic Press, 1993.

CPSIA information can be obtained
at www.ICGtesting.com
Printed in the USA
FFOW03n1608170617
36712FF

9 780692 780817